# CULTURE, CASH AND HOUSING

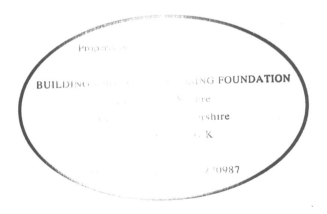

# Culture, Cash and Housing
## Community and Tradition in Low-income Building

MAURICE MITCHELL and ANDY BEVAN

VSO/IT PUBLICATIONS 1992

VSO
317 Putney Bridge Road, London SW15 2PN, UK

Intermediate Technology Publications Ltd
103–105 Southampton Row, London WC1B 4HH, UK

© VSO 1992

ISBN 1 85339 153 0

*Cover Picture: The Kasapa Brick making Co-operative in Zambia*

British Library Cataloguing in Publication Data

Mitchell, Maurice
    Culture, Cash and Housing: Community and
    Tradition in Low-income Building
    I. Title   II. Bevan, Andy
    307.7

    ISBN 1–85339–153–0

Typeset by J&L Composition Ltd, Filey, North Yorkshire
Printed by SRP, Exeter

# CONTENTS

# ILLUSTRATIONS

page

viii

# Preface

This book would not have been possible or be of any value without a certain accumulation of experience in the field. While we seek to address a wide audience of builders, planners, architects and community workers, both in the North and in the South, we quite consciously offer, in the main, the experience of VSO volunteers as food for thought. Naturally, we have tried to generalize from this in a way which is intended to be of interest to many people who are unfamiliar with the particular development agency which has commissioned this work. We also hope that this book will stimulate further discussion, criticism and development of ideas.

# Introduction

Some words on how the book is presented, explaining its structure, may help the reader at this stage. The book is divided into two parts: one on theory and the other practice, with a good deal of overlap and inter-weaving between the two.

Part One consists of two chapters, the second of which is divided into three major sub-sections. Chapter One, 'Why We Build', gives some general background, and an introduction to historical and developmental issues underlying the building process in a wide variety of societies. Overall, it sets the parameters for the subjects we tackle in the book as a whole.

Chapter Two, 'Choice of Building Design', aims to provide a more rigorous theoretical background to development work in the building field, surveying the literature on the subject. In its three sub-sections, chapter two examines:

○ Traditional building in a traditional context
○ Changes — specifically related to urbanization, the spread of a cash economy, and the availability of new materials, and
○ The roles of government and other national structures in those changed circumstances.

Proceeding from the considerations of theory outlined in Part One, part two sets out some propositions on practice. These appear as 'Guidelines for development workers and agencies' in Chapter Three.

These guidelines have not been plucked out of thin air. They represent a theoretical summary which draws on diverse building traditions built up and refined from the practical work of generations of people, all over the world. In addition, these guidelines draw on the more experimental work of the building research stations which has gathered momentum as the pace of urbanization has quickened.

More particularly, this book says something about the experience of VSO builders — a group of people who happen to have grappled with the changing circumstances outlined in Chapter Two — in the context of development work. Their story is told in chapter four, which presents a series of case studies.

A word or two is in order here on the scope of the case studies. Over the last 10 years, there has been a steady growth in the size of VSO's technical programme. Within the technical programme, a significant number of volunteers over the last few years have been involved in low-income building projects or community-based building projects of one kind or another, as planners, architects, site supervisors or builders.

Naturally, we feel it is important to evaluate the work which has been done by these volunteers, so that lessons can be learned by new volunteers going overseas in the future and by other practitioners of building, especially those who live and work in southern countries, or who believe, as we do, that the lessons learnt from community-based building are of great use to builders and planners everywhere.

Many of the lessons gained by field workers in the last few years have been learnt the hard way, without the benefit of recorded prior experience. This book is intended to address this problem of the lack of recorded precedent. It also aims to put this prior experience within a theoretical background sufficient to enable development workers to apply this knowledge to their own contemporary projects.

In turn, we would like to encourage contemporary development workers to record their experience. By recording and analysing their time in the field they can contribute to the development of theory and pass their knowledge on to future generations of development workers.

It is only by pooling the experience of individuals that we can all learn from a wider experience than our own. With this in mind, we should remind our readers that Chapter Four, entitled 'Experience In The Field', is built up from the field reports of only 68 volunteers who have worked in the building field since 1987. There have been many other building volunteers in that time but there was only sufficient data in the records to support the case studies given. As is often the case with technical people, field reports from builders have tended, on the whole, to be brief, witty and cryptic, rather than comprehensive. Sometimes we get the impression that they felt that their technical reports would not be understood or appreciated enough by field staff or head office staff in London. At any rate, we hope that this small book will help to convince development workers, whatever agency they work for, that it is possible to learn from their work experience.

In addition, we've dug deep and looked at some pre-1987 reports too. Most important of all, we've spoken directly to a number of volunteers who happened to have been contactable while this book was being written, some of them when they returned home and, in a few very valuable cases, while they've still been at work overseas.

On the other hand, some countries feature more than others, for example Kenya, where there's been a very large technical programme in recent years and where VSOs field office has promoted the outlook of appropriate technology and sustainable development with particular enthusiasm.

Certainly, if this book falls into the hands of returned volunteers, or others, who feel that we've missed out or skimmed over some interesting or enlightening examples, please write to us. Evaluation needs to be a continuous process if our work, overall, is to improve and if we are, as a building community, to learn.

We hope that readers will cross-refer between the guidelines in chapter three and the experience in chapter four.

Chapter Five presents a summary, or checklist, for community-based builders. It is presented conditionally, that is with a strong warning on the need to consider fully the specifics of each and every situation. There is no standard workable approach. What we offer is advice in the form of a checklist of issues.

Finally, there are some conclusions, an appendix on the use of prototypes, a postscript and a full bibliography.

One other introductory word of warning is perhaps advisable. If we are interested in sustainable development, our verdict on this or that project will need to be conditional in most cases. By definition, it only emerges in the long-term whether a particular innovation is really sustainable. In many of the cases we look at, we may end up, in effect, pointing out that 'this is interesting, it shows real possibilities . . . but it's still too early to tell.'

There has been a long-standing commitment to the idea of sustainable development within VSOs technical programme. This is an approach which rejects the idea that we should seek to impose solutions (and especially not new, high-tech solutions which create long-term dependency on expensive, imported spares and know-how) on Third World communities. Rather, we believe that local people are the only ones who can reliably identify their own problems. To become sustainable we need to work with them and to their definition of needs and priorities. We may together be able to find ways to use the existing skills base, locally-available materials and low-cost, sustainable technologies as the basis for solving those problems in a way which will not be dependent on outside help, but will be adopted and maintained locally.

A growing understanding of the importance of the issues covered in this book is surely essential for any builder or planner who is going to make so bold as to try to make a contribution to building anything in someone else's back yard. We hope that this book will serve to reinforce that message.

ANDY BEVAN
MAURICE MITCHELL
*London, March 1992*

# PART I
## *Theory*

# CHAPTER ONE
# *Why We Build*

Over many thousands of years, human societies have tackled the basic problem of providing shelter in a wide variety of ways, adapting to the natural environment and making use of the materials it provides for the construction (or adaptation) of sheltered space. The most basic motive for building has been to provide shelter for a defined kinship group, often within a clearly marked, protected area.

The purposes of shelter include protection from the extremes of climate, heat, humidity, rainfall, snow, dust and wind. They also include personal or group security. Again, because humans are supremely social creatures, shelter is normally a focus for social living, for the raising of the very young, for the care of the very old, for the preparation and storage of food, for rest and for sleep.

Normally, the individual human dwelling is part of a settlement. Where more than a single small kinship group has settled, communal space (or communal buildings) between kinship shelters will be used in different ways and communal problems of health, water supply and waste disposal will have to be solved, especially in more densely populated societies.

Over and above the provision of basic shelter for the individual kinship group, there may be communal building projects. In some early societies of the Neolithic and early Bronze Age, it is remarkable that the most impressive, permanent 'buildings' — often erected with vast, collective effort from durable and massive materials — were communal. In cultures based on, for example, shifting agriculture, where a clan might revolve and move around a large territory, large and elaborate burial cairns might be built in a place central to the whole territory, emphasizing the continuity of the clan's relationship with the whole of that territory. In such ancient examples, we see the beginnings of an architecture which is not purely functional, but which has artistic and cultural dimensions too.

A development worker is unlikely to be involved in deeply traditional matters such as communal facilities for burial and ceremonial. However, we should consider other public facilities, whether communally or individually held, which provide a productive or servicing role for the community at large, from the village corn mill of mediaeval England or the posho mill of rural Tanzania, to municipal government buildings, health facilities and huge places of employment now to be found in every city in the world.

Certainly, in this book, we will look at development projects involving the construction of amenity buildings, such as schools and clinics, as well as the construction of dwellings. In particular, we will examine the training role of amenity building projects, where new methods and skills are introduced to a community, and the demonstration and evaluation effects too — studying which, if any, features are adapted and adopted by the local people in their own building work.

All of these problems form part of the recurring and developing pattern of human settlements and the provision of shelter. Our prime concern here, however, is to focus on the problem of housing need, that is the provision of dwellings.

## A survey of housing need

Clearly, the provision of shelter, and the steps taken by human societies to meet their housing need, has changed through thousands of years of history. Changing climate, due to ice ages, desertification, and consequent changes in the availability of plant and animal products, such as timber and hides, are cases in point.

The biggest problems, however, and the ones which we will focus on, are the changes in methods of housing provision brought about as a result of an increase in the sheer scale of housing need.

While considerations such as the continuing availability of traditional materials may be an important challenge in specific cases, the real problem of housing provision in the so-called developing world in the last quarter of the twentieth century is one of population increase. In that context, there are other important factors. They include urbanization, planning controls and changing expectations.

All of these things produce pressure for change in housing design and construction methods. The range of levels of pressure needs to be borne in mind. Pressure can vary from gradual change within the context of continuing village construction methods to the kind of rapid shocks which are forced on a community, for example by natural disasters.

When considering these factors, we need to bear in mind the simple fact that the problem of housing provision and the meeting of housing need is not only the result of increasing demand for the number of housing units. We also need to remember that any rise in socially-determined housing standards, making each unit more expensive (in terms of time and resources) to construct and maintain, also adds to the size of the task.

## Population increase

This is not the place to set out all the arguments about the causes of population growth in the developing world. Even so, if we are to grapple with the question of housing need, we need to look, however briefly, at the population pressure behind it — and to note that it is a particularly concentrated form of pressure in the less developed countries.

4

During the Industrial Revolution of the eighteenth and nineteenth centuries, the human population of the British Isles grew rapidly. It almost doubled between 1760 and 1820. The advances of the Agrarian Revolution meant that agricultural output developed rapidly at more or less the same time but it was still necessary for Britain to resort to massive grain imports. This, in turn, was only possible because Britain could rely on a vast world trade, resting on a colonial empire with cheap raw materials and captive markets guaranteed. Needless to say, this combination of circumstances is simply not available to developing countries in the late-twentieth century.

Sometimes, the presentation of a population crisis would lead us to believe that chaos is confined to the South. This is simply not true. In reality, we should stress that the changeover from a predominantly agrarian society to an industrialized one, from a traditional to a completely cash economy, was a traumatic one in Britain, and in the rest of northern Europe. For example, in Britain and Ireland we should not forget the massive disruption and chaos of the Scottish Highland Clearances, of the Irish potato famine (and the starvation and mass emigration which it caused), or of the urban squalor, plagues and epidemics of early industrial England, or of child labour in the 'satanic mills'.

In North America, of course, the replacement of traditional society by a modern, commercial economy involved the genocide of the indigenous population, the transporting of an estimated 24 million Africans in slavery — with the deaths in transit of up to a third of them — and, later, mass exoduses of huge poor populations from northern, central and southern Europe. Maybe we should bear these things in mind when we examine the present difficulties facing developing countries in their transition from predominantly traditional, agrarian societies to predominantly urban ones.

In the developing countries, it is true that this transition has been even more marked. It has also been complicated by the fact that the countries which are already industrialized control the world market and insist on putting their own special priorities first.

Since 1900, world population growth has accelerated. As the century has worn on, this growth has shifted more and more to the less-developed countries too. Miles Litvinoff (1990) summarizes the position this way:

Humanity reached its first billion in about 1800, its second in the 1930s, its third in about 1960 and its fourth in the late 1970s. Now carrying 5.3 billion people, the earth will be home to a further 90 million-plus each year until the century's end . . . It is a mistake to think that human numbers are a problem for the poor countries alone. Japan, the Netherlands and the UK are more densely populated even than China and India, while Africa and Latin America are the emptiest continents. Besides, during their lifetime, children born in the North have a much greater impact on the world's resource base and environment than their counterparts in the South.

5

Why have human numbers risen so fast? The reason is partly mathematical since each expansion creates a larger accumulated total on which the next expansion is based (exponential growth). But the percentage rate of increase has been rising too. The likely worldwide rate of population increase was around 0.3 per cent per year in the seventeenth century, taking 250 years to double. By the 1970s, annual growth was 2.1 per cent, doubling every 33 years (Meadows, Randers, Behrens 1972).

To sum up, one of the net effects of this burgeoning population growth, especially in the countries which can least afford to improve infrastructure, is to create a huge need for more housing.

## How does urbanization affect this picture?

So population is increasing dramatically all the time. Even so, if the overall pattern of living and the spatial location of settlements remained unchanged (that is, mostly rural), solving the housing problem would simply depend on the availability of more of the traditional building materials and skills.

More people would mean more pressure on the land, but as long as the production of food could be increased sufficiently (through improved methods, more land under cultivation, and the like) the problem of building houses could probably be solved by simply increasing traditional house building, using tried and tested methods. Maybe there would be scope for more specialization. For example, some people could give up farming part-time or full-time to specialize as builders for their neighbours. Perhaps there would be pressure for more durable dwellings which needed less maintenance, so that farmers could farm more intensively and be freed from the need to repair roofs and walls so frequently. But, overall, it would probably be possible to envisage a gradually evolving response, using traditional techniques and materials, emerging within a traditional, rural society.

Of course, we could not ignore pressures such as erosion, overcropping, deforestation and desertification. All of these, as well as affecting food production, would also affect the production of traditional building materials like timber and thatch. The traditional house is as much an agrarian product as the crops and livestock which depend on a balanced ecological system.

In the real world, though, this model of an unchanged pattern of life is of little relevance. The reality is that population increase goes hand in hand with a process of urbanization. This involves the growth of urban centres at a number of levels, from small urban centres to huge mega-cities. Hardoy and Satterthwaite (1989) have drawn attention to the fact that big Southern cities in the late 1980s may not have been growing as fast as was predicted 10 or 15 years ago. But, whatever the debate about how fast they are growing, urbanization continues apace.

Generally speaking, the larger the urban agglomeration, the more intense and complicated the housing problem becomes. However, as Hardoy and

Satterthwaite point out, we should avoid thinking in terms of a rigid rural/urban divide. Many networks based on rural life continue to exist in the big Southern cities and many rural skills and attitudes of self-help and communal action contribute to the solutions which are actually being found right now to the problems of urban housing.

## Urban centres

Most new housing and most new neighbourhoods in such cities are organized, planned and built outside the law. Most urban citizens have no choice but to build, buy or rent an illegal dwelling since they cannot afford the cheapest legal house or apartment . . . In most cities seventy to ninety-five per cent of all new housing is built illegally.

Hardoy and Satterthwaite (1989)

Within the limits of every urban centre in the developing world, there are two separate cities; an official city which is registered, highly regulated, taxable and legal; and an illegal, unofficial city. As the quote above suggests, nearly all new housing is taking place in the second type of city. Even where new, low-cost housing initiatives take place within the domain of the official city, then, by definition, it is the middle-class and not the poor who seem to benefit.

In the genuinely low-cost, high-density, illegal settlements of the majority, unassisted by officialdom and its regulations, new types of housing problems — which differ greatly from those found in a traditional, village setting — have to be solved, on a self-help basis. There are problems of scale and of intense overcrowding. Traditional fuels may be unavailable or inappropriate. Fire-control, drainage, sanitation, water supply, power supply, security, first-aid, health and hygiene, and educational provision are all problems to be solved on a new scale. But over and above all of them, and preceding all of them, is the fundamental problem of access to land.

The squatter settlements of most cities are often to be found on steep hillsides, swampy low-lying land, landfill sites, beside large open sewers or in noisy areas such as those near industrial sites or airport perimeters. Health and safety factors, even such elementary ones as avoidance of land which is prone to landslides or occasional flooding, will probably be outweighed by the simple need to find a place to live which is close to the possible places of formal or informal means of earning a living.

Despite the fact that they are usually forced to occupy the least suitable building land, security of tenure is rare. Even so, the self-help tradition of the villages, making use of locally-available materials to build one's own dwelling — maybe with the help of one or two specialist artisans — is adapted to the new, urban environment. Squatters build their own homes, using and re-using discarded industrial packaging, pallets, sheet-metal, oil-drums, or whatever else comes to hand.

7

Over a period of time, they may come together to put collective pressure on municipal authorities to provide services such as rubbish collection, drainage, sanitation, water supply and education. Indeed, in many cases, squatters may organize to carry out a planned occupation of an identified area of land, even before any dwellings are built.

However, if squatters live in permanent fear of having their homes bulldozed, there is little incentive to work collectively at long-lasting improvements or permanent upgrading. This is one of the fundamental problems. It is compounded by the problem of regulations. In most cases, formal building regulations bear no relation to the economic and social realities of these high-density settlements, and actually form an obstacle rather than an encouragement to improvement and upgrading.

For example, the head of a poor family may eventually find a permanent job and a reasonably steady income. The family may then wish to erect a more permanent home, possibly made of stabilized earth blocks instead of recycled, makeshift materials. But they will find, more often than not, that these improved building materials still do not pass the strict building regulations of the city concerned. If materials do not meet the standard there is no hope of securing a bank or building society loan. Equally, a family may wish to build a small two-room apartment at first, building within their means, aiming to add further rooms, a latrine block and other facilities, at a later date. Again, however, it will usually find that the regulations do not cater for this pragmatic and realistic incremental approach, but insist on a finished house which meets all the building code's requirements at once.

A fundamental contradiction seems to exist here between the positive self-help approach of the squatter citizens and the rigidly framed but unrealistic planning and building controls. How has this contradiction come about?

**The origin of planning regulations and building standards**

In the West, public health, building control and planning regulations originated as a response to the urban squalor and the typhoid, cholera and tuberculosis outbreaks of the early phases of industrialization and urban living or, indeed, to loss of life in urban disasters, such as major fires or the collapse of large structures. In most cases, they reflected democratic pressures within a society which was already predominantly urban. (In passing, we should note that, even during the mass housing drive of the Victorian era in Britain, the efforts of the private sector, the charitable housing trusts for the poor, and company housing measures were complemented by a considerable degree of self-help, for example through savings movements.)

In general, the planning, building and public-health regulations of that era reflected the needs of a highly urban society at a given stage of economic development. In the main, it was these self-same standards, with marginal adaptations for tropical conditions, which were introduced by colonial administrators into urban areas in the colonies in the first third of the twentieth century (for example, Nairobi Municipal Council's Building and Planning Regulations of 1926).

However, these regulations applied only to the central or wealthy suburban areas frequented and inhabited by the Europeans. They were deemed to be appropriate to the needs of this same small elite and reflected the social and economic possibilities open to that elite. These regulations did not apply, and were never designed to apply, to the majority of the people.

In the double standards of European and non-European areas and controls, we see, in most cases, the origins of the official and the unofficial city, and the inappropriateness of colonial regulations for solving the mass housing problems of the urban poor of developing countries today. Even where this problem is fully recognized by the planning community — or even by the national government of the country — it may prove to be very difficult to overcome inertia, inherited attitudes and conflicting professional interests in rewriting and simplifying these regulations.

For example, a major seminar entitled 'Building By-Laws and Planning Regulations' was held at the Milimani Hotel in Nairobi, 27 and 28 November 1990, sponsored by ITDG (Intermediate Technology Development Group) and hosted by the Ministry of Lands and Housing and the Housing Research and Development Unit of the University of Nairobi. The consensus view of all present was that existing building regulations are inappropriate to the real needs of urban development in modern Kenya and that, in particular, some of the standards were so unrealistically high that they were an obstacle to the promotion of policies of urban improvement and low-cost housing provision.

Even so, the seminar proceedings revealed that the Ministry of Health had felt duty-bound, because of existing legal provisions regulating building, to take court action against a new housing scheme at Nyahururu because it proposed to install dry pit latrines — forbidden in a recognized housing scheme in a municipality — as a reasonable, low-cost alternative to high-cost sewerage. In fairness, it should also be pointed out that there are examples from Kenya, such as the large Koma Rock low-cost housing scheme in Nairobi, where a more imaginative, flexible and well co-ordinated attitude to the application of relevant building standards has been displayed by the various government departments.

### Self-help in an urban context

Self-help is the only viable route for most people in solving their housing problems in the cities of the South. Most newcomers to urban life bring with them a self-build tradition. In its original, rural context, this tradition may be very conservative, rooted in custom and deeply traditional.

In the urban context, however, self-build is forced to become much more inventive and innovative, using new materials and solving new problems of scale and complexity, often involving sophisticated co-operation with neighbours in the fields of building and social action. One of the real challenges of the 1990s and the first years of the next century will be to find a planning approach which is able to raise standards of housing and public health by working with that self-build tradition, rather than working against it.

We develop these points more fully in chapter two, but, almost certainly, this approach will utilize the following measures:

○ *acceptance of the value of an incremental approach* to urban self-built housing, that is allowing people to build a minimal one- or two-room dwelling initially, if that is all they can afford, and planning to allow space for additional building (at the back or side of the lot, or a second storey if adequate foundations have been laid);

○ *guaranteeing security of land tenure* as the best way of encouraging self-help upgrading of dwellings and communal areas and services. (Note: successful schemes for land-share as an alternative to eviction of squatters exist in a number of countries, notably Thailand); and

○ *use of site and services schemes*, with municipal authorities concentrating on the provision of pedestrian access, drainage, sanitation, lighting and water supply for self-build communities. This is a positive alternative to squandering scarce resources on complete building of estates which will be so expensive that they will only be accessible to the relatively wealthy few and probably located too far from work (formal or informal) for the poorest sections of the population.

### Changing expectations

People may decide to improve or change the type of dwelling which has been traditional. In a word, they may opt for an improved quality of housing, as well as being interested in the sheer quantity of housing available.

In chapter two, the factor of change is dealt with more comprehensively (see pp. 33–54). Here, we merely want to note that changing expectations which involve more time and resources being expended on housing provision, will add, at least in the short term, to the total problem of housing need. It may also, of course, add to the durability of the total housing stock and may therefore reduce the need for rebuilding and maintenance in the medium to long-term.

So, in addition to officially enforced regulations which have an impact on housing standards, we need to consider the straightforward, socially-determined aspirations of people for better housing. These aspirations would include those arising from education or new perceptions of the need for improved health and sanitation (for example, smoother, and therefore easier to clean, surfaces for walls and floors, chimneys to take away smoke, roofing materials which discourage infestation and which permit rainwater catchment to provide more and better water, and so on).

Other innovations may arise from changes in family size. This could be as a result of more children surviving or, on the other hand, through smaller nuclear families replacing larger, extended families. Again, political factors may play a big part. For example, immediately after independence in Tanzania, many women and children, who had been banned from the urban areas, came to Dar es Salaam to join their husbands. Changes of this kind will clearly lead to a new demand for the type of house required, with considerations of size, internal divisions, and so on.

Equally, a demand for change may arise through straightforward emulation and a desire to copy a preferred style of house, usually with a higher status. This is not always an unmitigated advance. For example, the replacement of thatched roofing by corrugated iron roofing is definitely a case of pros and cons. On the positive side there is less maintenance, the possibility of rainwater catchment, fire-proof, and much less infestation. But on the negative side, a corrugated roof can be dangerous in high winds, have poor thermal characteristics, and be noisy in heavy rain.

With all of these innovations, however, in practice it will often be difficult for the householder to put forward a clearly thought-out case for adopting the change. It is most likely to be a case of a combination of a large number of reasons — often stemming from new possibilities arising from the advent of a cash economy and the new technical options which it makes available outside the traditional sector. Without the availability of cash, for example, thatch provided on the self-help, mutual-obligation, trade-by-barter, payment-in-kind basis will be more likely to continue in widespread local use than the shop-bought corrugated iron sheeting.

We examine the issues of traditional building, and the factors which may arise within a community to promote change in the traditional built environment, more fully in the chapter which follows.

## CHAPTER TWO

# Choice Of Building Design

## TRADITIONAL BUILDING: VERNACULAR ARCHITECTURE

In order to understand the range of complex issues covered in the last chapter, relating to the change from vernacular building to urbanization and government intervention, it is useful to start again and ask what do we mean by traditional building, and to what changes are we referring?

Perhaps we are naïve to assume that traditional buildings reflect a society in harmony with its environment. But, after all, such buildings represent the accumulation of centuries of assimilated wisdom in the techniques of transforming local materials into shelter for the community. Since the 1960s, authors such as Denyer (1978) and Brunskill (1978) have attempted to classify and define the various aspects of traditional, or vernacular, architectures and to capture this essence of harmony and the notion of continuous steady development. Such notions are often used as the starting-point for criticism of housing today.

It is particularly in considering the basic requirement for shelter in the community that the concept of harmony with the environment has been considered appropriate. After feeding and clothing ourselves, we have and always will, so the story goes, build a shelter, using materials which are immediately available, and using techniques which we have learnt from previous generations.

Turner (1972) has demonstrated that housing is not just a product in that it is a roof over our heads, four walls and a door. It is also a process which is fundamental to the cultural well-being of the society within which and by whom it is constructed. In Turner's terms, housing is not only a noun but, more importantly, a verb. Thus, the process by which a society builds its dwellings (the way they are designed and the involvement of the society in their construction) is at least as significant as the efficiency of the house as a product providing protection from the elements.

Contemporary housing design and construction is a much more rapid, complicated and often more disjointed affair than the slow evolution of form which characterizes the traditional housing process. Authors such as Rapoport (1969) and Oliver (1971) have sought to define those factors which influence traditional housing form so we may better understand the changes which have followed.

Obviously, rapid and abrupt change is nothing new. The fortunes of empires and cultures have risen and fallen again. In such circumstances,

12

tradition may not always be a reliable repository of essential knowledge. Cement which will set under water was produced by the Romans but forgotten with their empire's collapse. Cements with similar properties were only rediscovered in the late-eighteenth century, culminating in the introduction of Portland cement in 1824.

In Turkey, earthquake-resistant construction details had been developed and incorporated within the building tradition during past decades of seismic activity. However, as there were no significant earthquakes for several generations, these details were forgotten and omitted from traditional vocabularies in more recent years. This lapse of collective memory within the building tradition had catastrophic results as a result of the 1970 Gediz earthquake (Oliver 1987).

Details of cyclone-resistant construction have similarly been expunged from traditional Vietnamese house construction. Here, wire or string ties which were traditionally cast into clay roofing tiles to ensure a firm fixing to the roofing timbers, were omitted in houses built during a generation of seasonal calm (Mitchell 1990). This increased vulnerability to Cyclone Irving in 1989. In these cases at least, tradition has not been a safe keeper.

Traditions which appear to have been gradually evolving from time immemorial, may in fact have been introduced relatively recently, and may be capable of integrating with or completely replacing previous traditions. In the late-nineteenth century in the western highlands of Cameroon, there existed a well-developed tradition of house construction using raffia-pole walls, tall, distinctive, beehive-shaped thatched roofs, and elegantly carved door frames. The German colonial authorities used experience gained elsewhere in Africa to introduce a system of earth-block walls and tiled, or simply thatched, roofs. Both systems employed local materials. But as forest products became more scarce and labour more expensive, the longer-lasting earth-and-tile houses quickly replaced the distinctive raffia architecture as the norm. Later, cheap imports of corrugated iron largely replaced the roofing tiles. More recently, cement was used to stabilize the earth blocks. All this for the purpose of providing more permanent buildings.

This transfer of building traditions by colonial authorities is nothing new. For a large part of its history, the wealth of the Islamic civilizations was based on the trade between east and west, which followed such camel routes as the Silk Road between China and Europe, and flourished until the advent of cheaper sea routes. Along these trade routes, merchants brought back stories of the comfortable dwellings of their hosts, and new notions of how this could be achieved back home. Conquerors brought back skilled trades-men who adapted their techniques to the new environment and produced demonstration houses which would be emulated by the less well-travelled members of the population.

In some circumstances, traditional building technologies have been transferred from one context to another. Until recently, traditional buildings in

Niger relied on the trunks of the Dom palm to provide beams for roofs and suspended floors. Desertification, following the droughts of the 1970s, has reduced the availability of such timber. As a result of a programme carried out by Development Workshop since 1980, vault and dome roofs built with uncompressed and unstabilized blocks, requiring no timber for form-work or in the finished structure, have become popular in many parts of the country. In some villages demand now outstrips the local masons' capacity to build for all their clients. This is a South to South transfer which has adapted and developed techniques which come out of those used traditionally in Nubia, Egypt, where the same basic structural techniques were re-popularized by the work and writing of Hassan Fathy in the period after 1940 (Development Workshop 1990; Hammer and Tunley 1991; Bullard and Tunley 1992).

When looking at past traditions in order to understand the future, it is easy to imagine a long, slow evolution to the present whilst anticipating exponential growth — often to cataclysm — in the future. In fact, the examples of traditional building which we see today are only those that have survived, either as long-lasting products or as oft-repeated processes, out of numerous other examples which have not.

It is to this somewhat imaginary concept of traditional architecture being always in harmony with its surrounding environment that we must now turn. If this concept is the measure of housing now and in the future, of what does it consist? Implicit is the proposition that the form of the traditional house, Turner's product, is affected, some would say determined, by the environmental context. There is also the additional proposition that the house should be constructed, extended, maintained and adapted (Turner's process) by its occupants, perhaps with the help of their extended family.

For the purposes of discussion, we have subdivided the environmental context as follows:

○ Climate
○ Techniques and materials
○ Social and cultural factors, and
○ Economy.

We will then go on to consider the process of housing and self-help in this idealized traditional context.

## Climate

Koenigsberger et al. (1974) have shown how the world can be divided into several distinct geographical areas where characteristics of temperature, rainfall and wind enable climate types to be defined. The tropics can be divided into the following four zones:

○ Warm-humid equatorial climate
○ Hot-dry desert or semi-desert climate
○ Composite or monsoon climate, and
○ Tropical upland climate.

The traditional model house provides shelter from extremes of heat, dust and rain whilst modifying outside conditions to provide thermal comfort inside.

*Warm-humid climates*
Warm-humid climates usually have two rainy seasons with very little difference between day and night temperatures. Comfort is provided firstly by protecting the inside of the building from direct solar radiation with a thick, insulated overhanging roof. And secondly, by ensuring a constant stream of ventilation to encourage cooling through the evaporation of perspiration. The form of the house will be single-banked, that is, having opposite walls open to the breeze. (This openness of the walls is often at odds however, with the need for security and privacy.) Steeply pitched roofs allow high volumes of air to circulate freely inside. Sometimes a verandah will surround the main rooms.

Highly-adapted structures from this zone can be as simple as the pole-and-thatch daytime shelters on the roadsides in rainforest areas. More sophisticated two-storey timber-framed thatched structures can often be found on the side of a hill to catch the wind. Heavy, steeply-pitched thatch overhangs the walls, shedding the heavy rain and reflecting the sun's rays. Here, the walls of the upper floor are open, providing a cool area for living or sleeping. The lower storey, constructed of solid masonry or earth, is used only for secure storage.

*Hot-dry desert climates*
Hot-dry desert climates are typified by lack of rainfall and large differences between day and night temperatures. There may be one short rainy season during which cultivation is concentrated. In this situation the careful storage of the one crop is given priority over other shelter needs. This contrasts with the warm-humid zone where crops are grown all the year round and food storage is less critical.

Traditional courtyard houses in north Africa and parts of the Middle East have been well adapted to provide comfort in hot-dry climates and there is an extensive literature on the subject (for example Al-Azzawi 1969). The walls and flat roofs of these houses are thick, with a high thermal capacity providing a reservoir to absorb the excessive heat of the day and return this during the cool night. A tall courtyard provides cool shade in the morning and evening. During the day, as the air heats up in the courtyard, it rises and draws hot air out of the rooms facing the courtyard. Openings

15

Figure 1. *Traditional two-storey house in a hot humid climate. Note that the earthen lower storey, used primarily for storage supports a comfortable, well ventilated upper storey carrying a thickly insulated thatched roof.*

on the outside however, are minimal to avoid glare, dust and solar heat gain.

Some houses are fitted with wind towers reaching up to cooler, less dusty layers of air as they pass overhead. They then direct this air down to damp basements or over wet charcoal to provide cool humid air in the courtyard. Unglazed earthenware jars full of water are strategically placed to humidify the internal atmosphere. Enclosed gardens are carefully cultivated to provide shade and humidity.

*Composite climates*
Composite climates are a mixture of hot-dry and warm-humid and contain traditional buildings which combine many of the characteristics described above. In Dubai, some houses have two wind tower/room combinations, one

built of cloth and bamboo with low thermal capacity, and the other of earth blocks with high thermal capacity. The choice of which room to occupy depends on the season. In Lahore, houses can be found with verandahs and multiple openings on the upper floors, in addition to thick-walled courtyards with their associated wind towers.

*Tropical upland climates*
Tropical upland climates are found in the high grasslands of such countries as Kenya, Ethiopia, Mexico and Colombia. They have large differences between day and night temperatures, at least one rainy season, and continuous, but slow, air movement. During some parts of the year, there is strong solar glare from a cloudless sky. But during the periods of cloud cover, perhaps just over half the year, solar radiation is diffuse.

Traditional shelters in tropical upland climates will employ some thermal capacity in their structure, to modify the extremes of day and night temperatures. Small openings help to keep out glare and dust. Depending on the rainfall, the roof will be either pitched or flat. Crop storage will be a priority. Usually these regions are pleasant and comfortable — daytime shelters are only required to protect the occupant from direct sunlight with

Figure 2.   *Modified traditional two-storey house in a hot humid climate, Ghana 1972.*

17

a well insulated (usually grass) covering. Dogon 'houses of speech' perched on cliffs on the bend of the Niger river in Mali are huge piles of millet straw simply supported on timber columns. They are sophisticated examples of shelters finely-tuned to be comfortable during the daytime (Duly 1979).

## Techniques and materials

Our model traditional house would be constructed of the materials found in the immediate vicinity, using techniques developed over previous generations. No centralized industry here, and no easy transport links by which materials plentiful in one region can be traded for those in another. Our notional traditional builder must construct a dwelling from the ground underfoot and the vegetation within carrying distance. Spence and Cook (1983) should be referred to for further reading on this subject.

### The ground underfoot

It is useful to analyse soil for building, according to particle size. The largest particles, stones, are the most durable of building materials, but require cutting to a usable shape, and transport can be difficult if large quantities are required. The smallest particles are those of clay. Intermediate sizes in ascending order are silt, sand and gravel. From these raw materials, traditional builders have made walls, and sometimes roofs, for as long as anyone can remember.

Figure 3. *Terraced house in a composite climate, China 1989. Note that the thick earth roof and walls, together with the chimney, suggest that extremes of heat and cold are modulated by their thermal capacity. At other times when the climate is hot and humid, comfort is provided by through ventilation.*

Figure 4. *Stone vaulted tomb-house in the Atlas mountains of Morocco. Note the so-called sacrificial coat of plaster has all but washed away.*

Let us look at the distribution of these materials. The earth is broken down by a number of forces acting upon it, but rainfall and ground water are the prime movers. Streams and rivers gradually wash mountains and uplands down to the lowland plains and the sea. The first particles to be deposited in this process are the heavier, rockier, sandy particles, and the last are the fine, dark sticky clays associated with delta areas.

Soil formation is also determined by climate and vegetation. The podzols of Russia and Scandinavia, formed under coniferous forest, tend to bog and peat. Under tropical rainforest however, where decomposition rates are higher, lateritic soils are found. These soils, a mixture of sand and clay, are the most naturally stable for building. They are found in Central America and the Amazon basin, large parts of sub-Saharan Africa, in parts of India and the Far East, and in north and west Australia. In its purest form, on exposure to air, laterite will irreversibly harden to provide an easily-shaped, hard building-block. Menard (1974) mentions that the Khmers used such bricks in the sixteenth century and that they are still used in Thailand today.

19

How does soil type affect the choice of walling material used by the traditional builder? It is the clay fraction of the soil which expands and contracts according to its water content. The clay allows it to be moulded to shape whilst binding the more stable sands and gravels together. This works well when forming the wall, brick or block, but can be disastrous if subsequent rainwater causes further clay movement leading to cracking and collapse. Thus the clay content of the building component should not be too large or too plastic.

Earth has a high thermal capacity and in hot-dry climates where excess daytime heat is stored in its fabric, for use during the cool nights, thick walls of desert soil with a high sand content are rammed between shutters. Houses up to six storeys high have been constructed this way in the desert region of Morocco. In the Asir mountains of Saudi Arabia, where there is a high rainfall, such structures need more than just an earth plaster protection. A thin course of flat stones is laid between each rammed-earth course, and projects from the face of the wall to shed rainwater.

Where the clay content is higher, blocks are more suitable than rammed earth, as these can be used more easily to produce thinner walls. Conveniently,

Figure 5. *Construction of a rammed earth wall in the Draa valley of Morocco, 1968.*

Figure 6. *Traditional house in the Asir mountains of Saudi Arabia, 1980s. Note the projecting stone between each course of rammed earth, used to shed rainwater away from the vulnerable wall surface.*

clayier earths are more often found in the warm-humid zone than in the desert. Thin walls, pierced with many openings, and requiring little or no thermal capacity, are appropriate in hot wet climates. Here, vulnerability to monsoon rains is reduced by regular maintenance of a sacrificial plaster coat, and large roof overhangs.

Where there are plentiful supplies of firewood or other fuel, and the soil is primarily clay of a low plasticity, bricks can be fired to form more permanent structures. These factors have combined to make fired-brick production widespread in parts of India where coal is usually available for burning in preference to diminishing fuelwood stocks.

A note of extreme caution should be sounded at this point regarding the conflicting needs for building materials and the requirement to conserve the natural environment. Whereas the traditional wood fuel-burning of bricks on a small-scale will allow the forest to recover, the large-scale reliance on

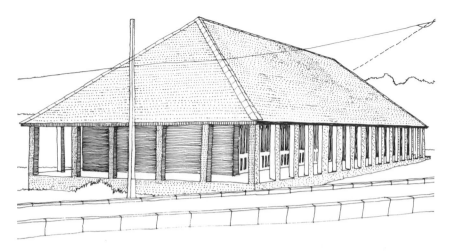

Figure 7. *Court house, Bamenda, Cameroon, built in the bungalow style, photographed in 1988. Plentiful local supplies of clay and firewood allowed the colonial authorities to construct this amenity building of long-lasting bricks and tiles.*

fuelwood for brickmaking unless combined with a sustainable planting programme is an untenable proposition.

*Vegetation within carrying distance*
Hardwoods and softwoods, palms, sisal (poles and fibres), grasses and bamboo have all been available to the traditional builder in forest and grassland areas. If regarded as renewable resources, questions of durability and competition with firewood use do not apply. Nor do competing demands from afar for forest products for foreign trade. Nevertheless, the traditional builder would have learnt that some species are more vulnerable to insect and fungal attack. His house form will have been developed from those possible, given the vegetation in the neighbourhood.

Whereas earth structures can only hope to give support in compression, timber can be used in bending and even in direct tension to provide the spanning elements of roofs and floors. Used in conjunction with earth-based materials, composite structures such as wattle and daub and reinforced earth are possible. In hot-dry desert regions there is great reliance on palm-trunk joists to provide the spanning element, combined with palm stems which span between the joists and support the beaten-earth floor or roof. In the past, in regions without such trees, earth vaults and domes had to provide the covering.

Timber-framed structures can be lifted off the ground out of the reach of flood-waters as in the case of the pile dwellings in Lake Nokwe in Benin.

22

Even grass can be used. Bundled together to form huge arches, and covered with mats, grass forms the houses of the marsh Arabs of the Tigris/Euphrates estuary (Thesiger 1964). Such houses are often dismantled and moved by canoe along the estuary waterways. The mobility of nomadic existence is reliant on the dismantling of tents or temporary shelters and their easy re-erection. Touareg shelters of bent saplings covered with mats are carried on camels or donkeys. The roofs of the more permanent nearby Hausa village houses are constructed from the same saplings bundled rather more substantially together and covered with earth.

Denyer (1978) provides a useful categorization of vegetable materials for African traditional architecture. She divides walls according to whether they

Figure 8.  *Thatched, oak framed house with wattle panels at Singleton Open Air Museum, United Kingdom. The main oak frame was pit sawn to rectangular sections and has lasted for several centuries with regular replacement of the wattle and daub panels. When such high quality building timber is not available the effort of pit sawing is often considered unjustified for short life timber framed structures; in this case, round pole timber is used, cut straight from the forest.*

23

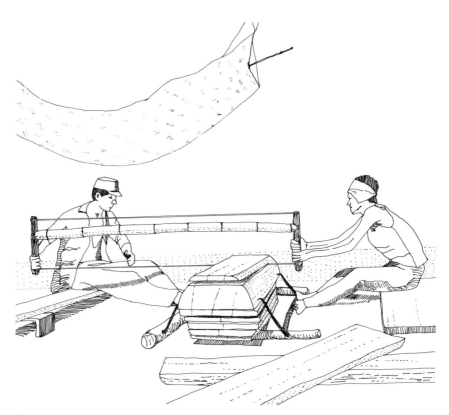

Figure 9. *Sawyers at work reducing logs to planks in Thanh Hoa, northern Vietnam 1990.*

are woven, tied to a framework, or planks arranged vertically or horizontally between upright poles. Thatched roofs are categorized as rectangular or circular. Earth roofs are categorized according to whether they are reinforced with a timber or bamboo framework, or unreinforced but thatched over.

The difficulty of cutting and shaping timber has limited the range of structures possible. Without powered circular saws, reliance on hand tools makes planks or any long length of rectangular-section timber enormously laborious to produce. Even assisted by pit saws, the reduction of large trees to manageable sections of building timber is a task which those used to buying suitable sizes off-the-shelf will find hard to imagine. For this reason, most traditional structures employ round-pole timber of a relatively short life. It is renewed as necessary from the surrounding forest.

Hand-sawing of tree trunks is still carried out extensively in northern Vietnam. Thanh Hoa, a provincial capital, displays an unusual mix of technology. Video film, television and camera shops trade side by side with workshops where sawyers work all day long to reduce logs to planks by hand.

24

Figure 10 shows a two-storey house constructed by its owner in the Torit region of the Equatoria province of Southern Sudan. The roof is thatched, the walls are of wattle and daub. In the foreground of the illustration stands another structure three storeys high, also built by the owner. Are these two structures traditional in the sense we have outlined above? They are both built of timber and thatch using hand tools, but both structures are quite different from the other dwellings in the village, which are typified by Figure 11. These other dwellings are, without exception, single-storey and circular, with conical thatched roofs and similar wattle-and-daub walls. Alongside is a granary with a woven, basketwork wall and similar conical roof which can be removed to gain access to the grain. It is raised off the ground to protect the contents from rats. The greatest care and skill has gone into the construction details of this granary as the protection of food is vital.

Figure 10.  *Unusual homestead, Torit region, Southern Sudan, 1977.*

The houses in Figure 10 are rectangular in plan, the first having a double-pitched roof. Large trees were needed for its towering neighbour — not just branches but whole trunks — requiring the felling of a larger number of trees than could be easily renewed in this savannah area. In contrast the circular buildings of Figure 11 do not appear to require the destruction of one complete tree. The conical buildings will need major maintenance after every rainy season and will probably be rebuilt every three to five years. The square buildings — particularly the tower — are expected to last considerably longer, with some maintenance. The effort involved in their construction is too great and the trees consumed too valuable to be associated with a short but renewable life.

The buildings shown in Figure 10 may be regarded as an extreme form.

Figure 11. *Traditional Mundari homestead (house and granary), Torit region, Southern Sudan, 1977.*

We will return to them later when considering the social and cultural influences on built form.

## Social and cultural factors

Rapoport (1969) regards socio-cultural factors as more important than climate or techniques and materials in their effect on house form. Once these other physical or functional factors are understood, then it is the aspirations of the inhabitants — restricted by what is acceptable — that has most significance. Even the most rigorous climatic conditions and limited availability of materials will leave some choices to the society as to how to house itself. And house form is probably the building type least determined by physical considerations. Religion, the make-up of family and clan, work processes and the intercourse of individual relationships are all expressed and symbolized by house form. Many choices are available, and different socio-cultural aspects will be dominant in societies with similar physical environments. Some societies, such as the Dogon who inhabit the Bandiagara escarpment on the edge of the Niger valley, use the form of both their houses and their settlements as a complex symbol of their idealized universe. Griaule, as quoted in Oliver (1971), demonstrated that the village may be laid out in oval form to represent the world egg. But it is also a person and must lie in the north–south direction. The smithy is the head and certain shrines the feet. The women's huts are the hands and are placed to the east and west.

The Gilbert islanders' fundamental world-view is that of an opposition between sea and land. Two of the corner columns of their houses are named after the gods of sea and land. The conflict of male to female is expressed by opposing rafters on either side of the roof ridge. Just as the roof could only be supported by both sets of rafters, so the society could only flourish with the co-operation of both men and women (Hockings 1987). Orientation of the house is frequently a cultural concern. Usually this will coincide with

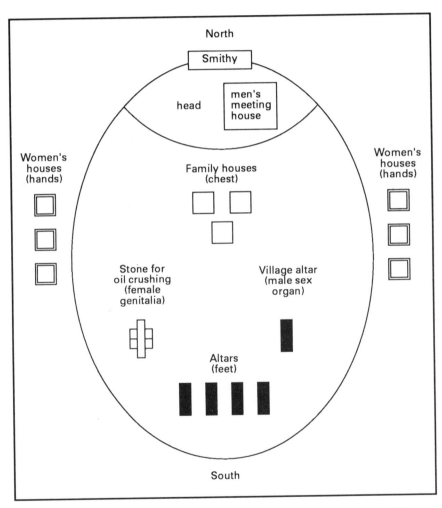

Figure 12.  *Diagram of the cultural symbolism of a Dogon village layout (representing the world egg) (after Griaule as described in Oliver 1971).*

climatic considerations. However, in the case of the Feng Shui rules for the determination of traditional form in China, if these cultural rules conflict with climatic factors, then the cultural rules predominate.

Thus, house form is used to extend and prolong the life of the ideals, values, attitudes and images, not of an individual but of the specific traditional society as a whole. A house is not only a physical object with functional attributes — it also reflects a traditional society's world view, ethics and codes of behaviour.

This may not be quite so true of modern societies, where social pressures and their expression in house form can be more individualistic. Modern social institutions can form alternative channels and barriers. They can replace to some extent, though not completely, the role of the traditional house in transmitting a society's values to its members. Bilbeisi (1990) has investigated the effect of sedentarization on the Bedouin nomad in Jordan. His work suggests that the fixed abodes of the new settlements do not offer quite the same formal symbolic certainty of cultural identity to their occupants as the named parts of yesteryear's nomadic tents. We will look more closely at the results of such changes later.

Rapoport divides socio-cultural influences into several categories which we might usefully consider:

○ Basic needs
○ Family
○ The position of women
○ The need for privacy, and
○ Social intercourse.

*Basic needs*

Breathing, eating, sleeping, cooking, playing and working — all these are basic activities which, according to the priorities placed upon them by the traditional society, can have a profound effect on house form. A society's attitudes to smells will affect the location of certain activities. Separation or combination of cooking and eating will affect layout. Sleeping customs will affect the use of furniture or mats. Some Japanese traditional houses are laid out using the dimensions of the tatami sleeping mat as the unit of plan form. It is not so much what is done — most societies carry out all the activities listed above. It is how and why these things are done which will be expressed in the cultural specifics of that society's dwellings.

*Family*

How is the family organized? Are its members monogamous or polygamous? Do the family eat together in the room of the grandfather as in certain Anatolian houses? Take the same area of northern Cameroon where polygamy is practised: in one society, the husband has a hut at the centre of the compound, surrounded by the huts of his wives; in another, he has no hut of his own but is obliged to visit the huts of his wives in turn. Suffice it to say that only by examining the specific family needs of a society can their effect on house form be understood.

## The position of women

Although this category is regarded as an extension of the last by many commentators, it is clear that the roles played by women have not been sufficiently recognized in the past. Moser (1987) divides these roles under the three headings of reproductive, productive and community management. Traditionally, spatial gender separation can often be found, as in the case of the Bedouin tent. This is often coupled with the pre-eminence of women inside the house or at least in those areas set aside for them. In Tinezouline, a traditional village constructed of rammed earth in the hot-dry Draa valley on the edge of the Sahara desert in Morocco, entrances are separated according to gender. The women's entrance is visually shielded from passers-by. Meeting-places are also gender-specific — wells for women, and the lobbies of main entrances for men. Again, the roles of women in each society may be expressed in the specific choice of its architecture.

## The need for privacy

In some societies, the threshold between public and private space occurs at the entrance to the house plot, whilst internally there is little or no privacy amongst family members. In others, there is a highly refined hierarchy of spaces — from public to semi-public to semi-private to private. In a crowded society, social defence-mechanisms operate against noise and visual intrusion. These are often reinforced by built form. Rapoport hypothesizes that the more crowded and hierarchic societies favour courtyard houses and the clear separation of domains.

In Hausa society the first building work entails the construction of a high wall around the plot to provide complete privacy, even if this means delaying the construction of rooms for lack of resourses. In contrast to this highly private form, there are many settlements in the surrounding savannah where only sleeping and shelter from the rain are indoor activities. The form of such a community is often described as permeable, to differentiate it from the hermetic (close-sealed) alternative described above.

The growth of permeable settlements starts with the smallest element which is the hut, and expands by means of more huts and fences until it meets with a neighbour or physical barrier. The settlement itself may have a barrier at its boundary for defensive purposes, but access to, and penetration of, spaces within the settlement is hardly determined by built form. The boundary between activities is flexible according to the needs of the moment. For example temporary restrictions on entrance to particular areas may be provided by symbolic fetish objects, and visual privacy may be provided by screens. The individual huts of these settlements, similar to that shown in Figure 11 are renewed every two to five years as the physical fabric decays. As this renewal proceeds, there is the opportunity for the land occupied by each family to be reassessed.

Whilst many view the issue of privacy in traditional societies as being primarily concerned with the position of women in society, it is in fact a highly complex affair.

*Social relations*

How and where do people meet: as individual to individual, as a family, as a clan or village? Market-places, coffee-shops and mosques clearly have their place. The young men and women of the Dinka cattle camps have for many years met once a week in the dry season for dancing in an open space on the outskirts of Juba in Southern Sudan. Courting couples in Hanoi have to book space with the authorities under particular trees in parks in order to spend time alone together in this crowded city.

How are guests received into the home? In some Islamic societies, guests are met in the entrance lobby and then shown to totally separate guest quarters. Other societies share all parts of the house, except the bedroom, with their guests. The nomadic Bedouin impart a high value to the sanctity of the tent as a haven for guests and are prepared to kill to protect the tent's honour if this sanctity is invaded. Nevertheless, tradition places a time-limit on such hospitality (Bilbeisi 1990). These social and cultural questions and their associated architectural expression are specific to each society.

Before turning to the issue of the traditional economy, we would like to return briefly to the example of the two homes shown in Figures 10 and 11 to discuss the socio-cultural expressions represented by their form.

Mundari society, to which the owner of the multi-storey dwellings belongs, practises polygamy. Here it is usual to build one conical thatched hut for each wife. Large villages are rare in this society. Individual homesteads and scattered hamlets housing one or two extended families are the more usual form of settlement (Barbour 1961).

At the time of the photograph from which Figure 10 is made, the house-owner was celebrating his third polygamous marriage. The tower house was to accommodate his youngest bride and to store his grain. The upper storey of the other house was for his second wife, and the ground floor of the same building for his first wife. Each wife required a higher room than the earlier wife in order to consent to marriage. The form of the two-storey building was an imitation of the Italian Catholic mission station building in a nearby village, which was a two-storey brick and sawn-timber construction. The climate, materials and skills were the same as the other Mundari dwellings in Figure 11. The world view, the aspirations and ideals of this householder, however, were clearly different and were expressed in the form of his buildings.

30

## Economy

In a traditional rural economy, agriculture predominated as the economic activity to which others, including house building, had to take second place. Construction would be carried out during seasons when agricultural activity was at its lowest. This was usually a highly co-operative and convivial activity. Families would combine in mutual self-help to erect each other's shelter. Given the restricted materials available, the level of skill required was often very high. As each building might not outlast a single generation, these skills had to be taught to each succeeding generation. This is a considerable task where there are little or no literacy skills. Where specialist building skills were required, these might be gender-determined or rest with particular family members. In Kenya, Kikuyu women thatch, whereas Kamba women don't. Any payment, even for more specialist skills which had to be bought in from outside the kinship group, would be paid for in kind rather than in cash.

Knowledge of a particular oily plant needed to produce a waterproof plaster from clay earth is a secret closely guarded by women in parts of Niger. Brickmaking outside Juba in Southern Sudan is carried out in the dry season by unemployed agricultural workers. This has always been the case, even though clay working is more difficult without abundant supplies of water, and despite unwanted cracking in unfired bricks being exacerbated by rapid drying.

Where traditional houses have a longer life, this is made possible by regular and intensive maintenance carried out so as not to interfere with the growing season. The fabric of the building is divided into the longer-lasting structural sections and the outer sacrificial coats of plaster which need to be regularly

Figure 13. *Traditional rammed earth houses in the Draa valley of Morocco, 1974. Note that all but the upper parts of the walls have had their sacrificial coat of earth plaster washed away leaving the structural rammed earth sections exposed.*

31

replaced if the building is to survive. Nowhere is this more apparent than in Zaria, northern Nigeria. There, quite sophisticated techniques have been developed to shed the rainwater from the flat-roofed earth houses and to protect the plinths. Many types of waterproof finish protect the walls, each with a specific known use and life (Daldy 1945). It is possible to suppose, in such a case, that if durability of fabric was important to Hausa society, then such houses might be regarded as permanent, having monetary value, and capable of being bought and sold. But this is not in accordance with the overriding concerns of the society, which are primarily cultural and based on changing family structure. Moughtin (1969) describes how:

Hausa families are of three types: individual families; a married man, his married sons and their dependants; or a group of collateral agnates [related on the father's side] and their dependants. These varieties of Hausa co-residential kin groups are not formal alternatives but manifestations of the same rhythmic and dynamic cycles. The effect of this household cycle is most evident in the organic nature of the settlement pattern. New family units are constantly being formed, maturing and breaking up. During the dry season each year, new homes are built. And during the rains, the unused parts of decaying compounds are reduced first to rubble, then to simple mounds of laterite. This process of growth and decay is assisted by the impermanent nature of the building materials. Once vacated, a building soon disappears, either naturally or by being demolished. Its materials are then reused for building on another site . . . In traditional Hausa society, land and the buildings erected on it have no market value, the ownership of the land being usufructuary only. The fabric of the house acts mainly as a shelter and is not regarded as a long-term investment. Until recently Hausa builders were not preoccupied with the durability of building materials.

There is a link here between the life-cycle of the traditional house, its maintenance or replacement, and the use of self-help labour for the collection of materials and the construction of the dwelling. The latter is linked, in turn, to the apparent total lack of any capital value for such buildings before the introduction of a cash economy. We will consider this further later, but another example will serve to illustrate the breakdown of traditional house form when cash payments are introduced for building work.

The Draa valley villages, constructed of rammed earth, were mentioned earlier. These villages, being regularly rebuilt and repaired, have lasted for hundreds of years. Traditionally, two skilled maalems are employed to build a house and to maintain it. The maalem is not only the builder, but also the repository of knowledge of climate, technology and culture for this building tradition. He decides how the needs of the occupiers are to be met. He also decides the layout, aspect and arrangement of the building and all the fine details of construction. Maalems are supported by up to 10 people from the family for the house, who gather materials and carry out the general labouring work (Mitchell 1969).

In the past, payment for a maalem's services have been full board and lodging for the duration of the work, plus a number of sheep and goats when the work is satisfactorily completed. Since the 1960s, maalems have been demanding payment in cash. They can, after all, obtain more lucrative employment in the factories of Casablanca. The families' cash income was at that time virtually non-existent and a lower level of maintenance of these buildings has obtained ever since. The number of skilled maalems is continuing to decline.

Consequently, alternative, more durable means of construction and repair for housing in this area are being sought by the Moroccan government. In this case, the complex skills handed down the generations rested solely in the hands of these skilled artisans. The people who employed them did not share these skills, and as the maalems become fewer so their buildings move towards terminal decay.

In such traditions, there is no separation between craftsman and professional. There were probably no drawings to work from and no modelling of the outcome for the future user to visualize his future dwelling. The builder knew what he was constructing because, with minor variations, he had done it many times before. There were also many examples at hand for discussing alternatives with his client.

In the next section, we will examine the impact of the relatively sudden changes which have occurred, not only in the type and durability of building materials, but also in moves to modernization and a cash economy.

## CHANGE

Christopher Alexander (1970) has proposed a useful model for examining the relationship between built form and context, and the effect of change on that relationship. Figure 14 shows this relationship. Alexander proposes that in the past there was a harmonious link between a building and its environment. Here we have the idealized view of tradition, which provided this link in the past. This was discussed in the last section. Small changes in environment are matched by equally small building adaptations which are carried out painstakingly by each subsequent generation. Recently, perhaps over the last century, or since independence from colonial regimes — it depends on your point of view — things have proceeded not by small change and approximation, but abruptly and irreversibly. Buildings have changed. Context, as represented by physical environment, techniques and materials, social and cultural aspirations, and economy, has also changed. Built form no longer fits the context like a glove. There is a mismatch. In Alexander's terms, we have moved from an unself-conscious culture to a self-conscious one.

33

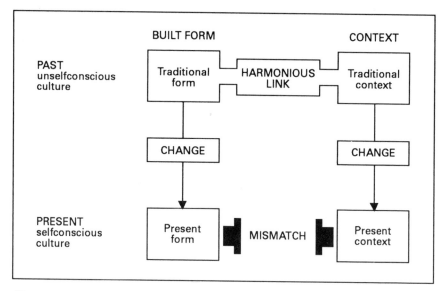

BUILT FORM             CONTEXT

PAST unselfconscious culture — Traditional form — HARMONIOUS LINK — Traditional context

CHANGE          CHANGE

PRESENT selfconscious culture — Present form — MISMATCH — Present context

Figure 14. *Diagram showing the effect of change on the fit between built form and context.*

Confusion reigns, so the theory goes. Traditional peoples, acquiring new ideas, are searching for built form to suit their new aspirations. City-dwellers are alienated by the ubiquitous, brash, reinforced concrete-framed blocks appearing everywhere. They yearn for the courtyard houses of their forefathers. Here Alexander sounds a note of caution. Yes, most definitely, both form and context have changed. But beware, unadapted traditional form is as unlikely to match the aspirations, changing ethos and world view of contemporary Kenyan society, for example, as are the unadapted imported European and North American buildings illustrated in glossy magazines.

So the search is on for cheap, low-income housing, well adapted to the climate and locally-available materials, for spaces which match the new living patterns, as well as for an expression of cultural identity in built form which is appropriate to contemporary ideals.

**Climate**

In a section discussing the changes in the factors affecting house form, climate is perhaps the joker in the pack. All in all, climate has probably changed very little over the last century. But there have been exceptions, and if the predictions on global warming are correct, these will continue and become more profound. In 1990, a joint policymaker's summary report of the United Nations Environment Programme on the Intergovernmental Panel on Climate Change (United Nations Environment Programme 1990) stated that:

34

The largest impacts on humanity of climate change may be on human settlement. The impact on developing countries, many of which lack resources for adaptation, may be particularly disruptive. Understanding likely impacts of climate change on human settlement . . . in such countries should be a high priority, together with reinforcing indigenous capability to design and implement strategies to reduce adverse impacts of climate change.

In the meantime, cataclysmic climatic events, named disasters by the United Nations, continue. The Sahel drought in the 1970s, for example, intensified the desertification of the region. It removed timber from the list of available building materials in many parts.

Earthquakes in Iran, Turkey, Mexico, Algeria and elsewhere necessitated a reassessment of the efficacy of traditional construction, and introduced new types. Such emergencies are thought to justify exceptional measures of intervention. Aiming to reduce costs and speed up delivery of temporary shelter, the West German Red Cross supplied standardized sprayed-polyurethane domes to the victims of the Gediz earthquake in Turkey in 1970. With similar aims, the Austrian government provided hexagonal prefabricated units. Both types of shelter were badly adapted to the climate. Moreover, they had been constructed without consideration for the way of life of the society for which they were made. Consequently, most of the victims preferred to construct their own houses out of the rubble of their old ones. Luckily for them, this rubble had not been cleared away by helpful aid agencies, as has been the case elsewhere. Those domes that were occupied needed to be adapted for extended family use. They required additions and extensions to fit in with cultural requirements. These additions increased their vulnerability to future earthquakes. All the victims interviewed would have preferred to have used the cash spent on these prefabs to have been available for self-help construction (Oliver 1987).

Building in areas where disasters (hurricanes, earthquakes, flooding and typhoons) are likely to occur is provoking the rapid development of a new body of knowledge which is related to the issues covered in this book. Whereas rapid, large-scale, emergency relief programmes usually hit the headlines, the careful gathering and dissemination of knowledge for the incorporation of sound construction, maintenance and use of buildings in these vulnerable areas together with advanced warnings made possible by satellite technology (in the case of typhoons) offers better if less spectacular protection.

Climate, so far however, is the least changeable of the factors considered. Its physics most clearly understood, it is also perhaps the most easily measured and described. The effect of shape, orientation and surface-to-volume ratio of overall form, the thermal capacity, and insulation and reflective properties of various building materials can all be given a relatively precise numerical value. Perhaps for this reason it was climate that was the first design variable that architects and engineers introduced into their schemes, when attempting to adapt building types imported from Europe and North America for use in the tropics. The very term 'tropical architecture', used throughout the immediate post-war years, illustrates the emphasis which was given to climate in influencing innovative house form during this period.

The work of Maxwell Fry and Jane Drew in West Africa and India illustrates this point. In their book (1964), Fry and Drew draw on the precedent of both traditional dwellings and the works of modern architects such as Le Corbusier. These illustrate how wall openings, roof insulation, overhangs, shading devices and landscaping can be used to modify the full range of tropical climates to provide internal comfort. They also give advice on the design of buildings in hurricane areas and on earthquake-resistant structures, and a little advice on the use of local materials. They give no advice, however, on meeting socio-cultural requirements.

More recently, concern has focused on the energy debate, which has addressed issues such as, how to ensure the most efficient use of energy at a time when the world's fossil-fuel reserves are seen to be clearly finite and their use polluting? Dwellings employ either passive methods or active systems, or a combination of both, to modify the climate. For example, traditional courtyard houses in Baghdad were seen as ideal passive modifiers. Thick earth walls modulate day and night temperatures. Courtyards induce ventilation, and hence cooling, using the stack effect. More active participation in the control of their thermal comfort is exercised by the occupants who open and close window-shutters and doors to control air movement at appropriate times of the day. Occupants also move to different spaces throughout the day as these spaces become comfortable — the roof at night and the damp basement in the heat of the day, for instance.

In current usage, passive systems act without plumbing or user control, while active systems transfer heat from one part of the dwelling to another, using pipework, transmitting fluid and pump, or by opening and closing shutters, or by moving insulation. All these alternatives require the involvement and understanding of the user. Viewing the debate from the energy perspective has produced new combinations of traditional and modern design. In the Centre for Ecological Development in Leh, Ladakh (part of the states of Kashmir and Jamal, North India), Michel Trombe walls have been successfully introduced. These have become very popular amongst house-owners as effective heating devices in the cool but sunny mountain areas (Schumacher 1987). Using the greenhouse effect, the sun's energy is trapped behind sheets of glass and stored in the wall behind. When required, air is encouraged to pass over the hot wall and is delivered to the room.

The superior thermal capacity of these earth walls, when compared to concrete for example, has led to a reappraisal of the value of this material.

In tropical areas it is much easier than in temperate zones for solar collectors to provide a fully operational, domestic hot-water supply. This can be as simple as an oil-drum filled with water, painted black, placed on the roof and fitted with a shower rose on the underside.

A degree of user involvement, perhaps even self-help, is required for active systems to be effectively maintained and controlled. Traditionally, it is argued, people had the time and understanding to open and close doors and windows and to move about the house. This was a pattern of social activity which was integrated into daily life. But things have changed, ways of life are different. A recent survey indicated that many wind-catchers in Baghdad had fallen into disuse as the occupants no longer knew how to operate them. Change is now more rapid in family need. For instance, the demands on the time of the user, in the technology of controlling active systems, is more extensive. This means it is not always possible for these techniques to be effective, unless the products associated with their success are fully integrated into the market system. To the extent that a house is an effective passive modifier, and the house form required to carry out that modification does not conflict with other attributes required of the form, then such a house will out-perform an air-conditioned box with a defective electricity supply. It will also out-perform a traditional house which is overcrowded and has been adapted and extended for an intensified urban life so that it can no longer function climatically as originally intended.

## Techniques and materials

Some of the most profound changes associated with the disruption of the traditional building process have been in the field of building materials and their associated techniques. Since the industrial revolution, stronger, more durable materials have been developed to replace earth, timber, thatch and bamboo. The introduction of Portland cement, steel and float-glass in the late-nineteenth century allowed new structural forms to be developed in the early twentieth. The widespread introduction of powered machinery to reduce timber to manageable rectangular sections, led to the invention of plywood, as well as to the destruction of the forests for export, and competition with charcoal-burners for domestic fuel.

### Cement

Perhaps the most important of these new materials is Portland cement. It has the property of setting under water, unlike lime and gypsum cements which need to react with air to harden. Cement is mixed with gravel and sand to form concrete. It can be reinforced with steel rods. Reinforced concrete is an extremely strong, durable and plastic medium with which to build. In many ways the availability of Portland cement in a developing country's building industry has been as important as water supply has been to its agricultural programme (Spence 1983). Cement is formed by heating a mixture of limestone and clay to a temperature of around 1500° Celsius. Such a temperature can only be achieved in a cost-effective manner at a plant large enough to process, say 300 to 5000 tonnes a day. As with all the other newly-discovered materials listed above, cash has to be paid for cement by the builder. In the early stages of a country's development the currency would have to be foreign exchange. The capital investment in both plant and distribution network is too high to be financed nationally.

New cement plants are usually given high priority in a nation's development programme. However, projects such as roads, bridges, dams and hydro-electricity usually take priority over housing when supplies of this valuable material are allocated. For this reason, building research stations, such as the Housing and Urban Development Corporation in New Delhi, India and the Building and Roads Research Institute in Kumasi, Ghana, have been attempting to develop alternatives to Portland cement. They have also investigated ways in which smaller quantities of this material can be used to build strong and durable buildings.

Sandcrete blocks are formed from a mixture of coarse sand and cement, either singly in simple moulds or by mechanized production in a jolt squeeze machine — these are the industry standard. In many situations, these have been replaced by landcrete or so-called stabilized earth blocks which employ smaller quantities of cement to provide the strength and durability required for domestic construction. A combination of the characteristics of the soil and different techniques is used to achieve this stability. The clay fraction of the earth provides some of the adhesion. In addition, the sand fraction of the soil is evenly graded from smaller to larger particles in order to reduce voids in the mix, since such voids would absorb cement ineffectually.

Voids are reduced still further by compressing the mix. The Cinva Ram machine was developed for this purpose by a Chilean engineer working at the Inter-American Housing and Planning Center (CINVA) in Bogota, Colombia. This is a simple device manufactured from mild steel plate. It consists of a mould box in which the soil and/or cement mixture is compressed against the lid from the bottom by a piston which is connected by a toggle linkage to a lever arm. While blocks produced in this machine are superior to those of unstabilized earth, they generally do not have the strength and durability of sandcrete blocks or fired bricks. The market for improved traditional materials which have increased costs, but still have such a specific quality range, needs to be carefully assessed before large-scale production is undertaken. This is confirmed by two of the case studies described in chapter four. After experimentation based at the Appropriate Technology Unit in Dang, Nepal a demonstration weaver's workshop was built at Tulsipur and well received by the local population. However, production did not proceed as the blocks were found to be too expensive for the domestic market and not durable enough for commercial buildings. In contrast to this, at Kusyokimanza in Kenya, a successful local blockmaking business was established as an offshoot of the building project at Muka Mukuu where the blocks were well received on the domestic market.

Building research centres such as the Department of Housing and Planning Research in Kumasi, Ghana, and Action-Aid Kenya, have adapted the Cinva Ram for use in their own country with varying degrees of success (Building Research Establishment 1982, Spence undated, Okie 1971, Action-Aid Kenya, undated). At the Building Research Establishment in the United Kingdom, a version has been developed which incorporates a pneumatic device for increasing the pressure on the mix. The walls of a medical clinic at Kabiro, in the district of Kawangare in Nairobi, were successfully constructed with blocks manufactured in this machine. The degree to which this new technology has been taken up, particularly in urban areas and in the so-called formal sector, depends on many factors, including the relevant building standards of the countries concerned. We will look at this more closely in the next section.

Others have worked on the replacement of Portland cement with other stabilizers, such as lime, which do not require such highly capital-intensive and centralized production techniques (Spence 1983). Small-scale lime kilns have been designed to be more efficient. The use of pozzolanic materials, materials which can be mixed with either Portland cement or lime to increase their efficacy, has been encouraged. Pozzolanas such as burnt, crushed clay powder — called surkhi in India, homra in Egypt and semen merah in Indonesia — have traditionally been used locally. Modern pozzolanas, such as pulverized fly-ash (PFA, residue from power stations) and calcinated bauxite waste, have been used to replace up to forty per cent of Portland cement in a mix.

Establishing the viability of these different types of cement is a question of assessing the capital and distribution costs, and comparing these with the quality of the product. Generally, centralization reduces production costs. However, it relies on a good distribution network, guaranteed markets and proximity to raw-material supplies. Decentralization, on the other hand, may increase production costs (Sigurdson 1977), especially if the market is small or transitory. On the other hand, it should reduce distribution costs.

The biggest difficulty with local production of building materials of any kind, particularly if they are produced on-site for one project only, is quality control. This is confirmed by the experience of development workers at the Glebe Skills Training Centre in St Vincent. The quality of the blocks produced to construct the centre was not maintained, and an attempt to set up a separate blockmaking business failed.

*Bricks and tiles*
The problem of quality control is nowhere more clearly evident than in the case of brick and tile production. In parts of India, where there are plentiful supplies of good-quality clay for moulding and coal for fuel, and where there

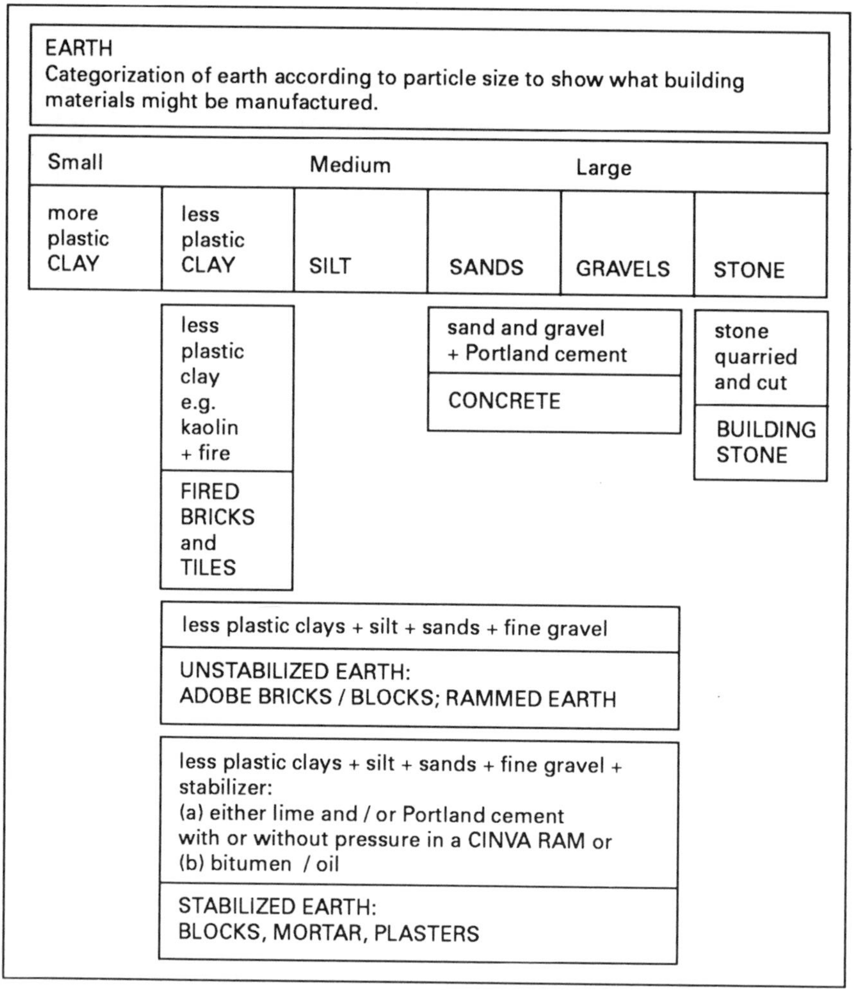

| EARTH Categorization of earth according to particle size to show what building materials might be manufactured. | | | | | |
|---|---|---|---|---|---|
| Small | | Medium | | Large | |
| more plastic CLAY | less plastic CLAY | SILT | SANDS | GRAVELS | STONE |
| | less plastic clay e.g. kaolin + fire | | sand and gravel + Portland cement | | stone quarried and cut |
| | | | CONCRETE | | BUILDING STONE |
| | FIRED BRICKS and TILES | | | | |

less plastic clays + silt + sands + fine gravel

UNSTABILIZED EARTH:
ADOBE BRICKS / BLOCKS; RAMMED EARTH

less plastic clays + silt + sands + fine gravel + stabilizer:
(a) either lime and / or Portland cement with or without pressure in a CINVA RAM or
(b) bitumen / oil

STABILIZED EARTH:
BLOCKS, MORTAR, PLASTERS

Figure 15. *Diagram showing the choice of earth-based building materials available from a given soil.*

is a guaranteed local urban market, such as on the outskirts of Madras, there is a thriving brick and tile industry. Bulls Trench kilns which are almost as efficient as the most modern kilns (Spence 1983) have been in use for generations, and product quality is high. Elsewhere the picture is not so good.

In Africa, the fuel used for firing bricks is usually firewood, which is a diminishing resource. The city of Juba, the regional capital of Southern Sudan, has upped and moved twice in its history, as supplies of firewood for domestic fuel became progressively further and further away. The

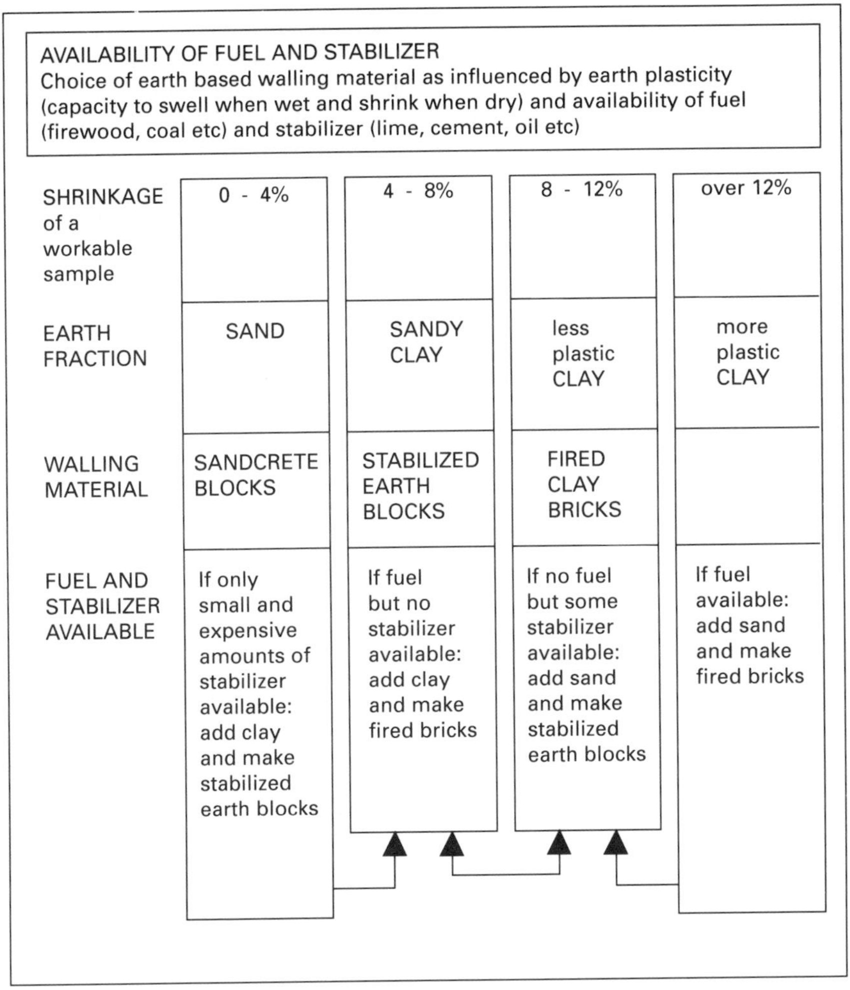

| SHRINKAGE of a workable sample | 0 - 4% | 4 - 8% | 8 - 12% | over 12% |
|---|---|---|---|---|
| EARTH FRACTION | SAND | SANDY CLAY | less plastic CLAY | more plastic CLAY |
| WALLING MATERIAL | SANDCRETE BLOCKS | STABILIZED EARTH BLOCKS | FIRED CLAY BRICKS | |
| FUEL AND STABILIZER AVAILABLE | If only small and expensive amounts of stabilizer available: add clay and make stabilized earth blocks | If fuel but no stabilizer available: add clay and make fired bricks | If no fuel but some stabilizer available: add sand and make stabilized earth blocks | If fuel available: add sand and make fired bricks |

Figure 16. *Diagram showing the relationship between choice of earth-based walling material and availability of fuel and stabilizer.*

introduction of intensive brick production has exacerbated this problem. Where the demand for bricks is low, investment in sheds to control the drying of the clay and produce a high-quality brick is more difficult to justify. The transportation of bricks and tiles by lorry over unmade roads is both expensive and likely to lead to breakages. Rules of thumb of 40 miles in Ghana (where the roads were asphalted), and 20 miles in Sudan (where they were not) were regarded as the maximum effective transport distance for bricks when competing with on-site production of stabilized soil blocks.

The Intermediate Technology Development Group, in the United

Kingdom, has sought to upgrade small-scale brickmaking technology over the last 20 years. It has looked at changing from slop to sand-moulding techniques, controlling the rate of drying, and developing improved clamp kilns. In order to overcome the problems of fired clay roofing tile production which include that of breakages in transit from factory to site, ITDG has also sponsored the development and production of fibre-cement pantiles. Projects using this technology are now functioning in a number of countries, including Kenya and Ghana.

*Timber*

We turn now to timber and recent changes associated with its use. Timber is a renewable resource. With careful management, it could still provide a most useful modern building material. It is easily worked and readily lends itself to cultural expression. Carpentry products can be found amongst the cultural artefacts of a majority of the world's societies.

The invention of the circular saw has made reduction of the tree to building lumber very much easier. Wholesale export of particular hardwoods has also been made possible. The best species are usually reserved for export by producer nations. Secondary species of lower quality are less valued by the population and cannot be fashioned to such a high degree of finish. They tend to be younger, less well seasoned and more susceptible to termite attack. In the Gambia, the Rhun palm, which had traditionally been used for roofing because of its termite-resistant properties, is now legally protected because of overcropping. In rural areas, competition continues with domestic charcoal-burners. In the towns, fear of fire is often given as a reason for restricting the use of timber.

Where powered saws are available, emphasis is usually given to the production of furniture, doors and windows, and roofing timbers. As most of the timber is low-quality short-grained hardwood, it is often difficult to obtain long straight regular sections. Sometimes, timber mills will only do the first cutting, perhaps producing only two or three section-sizes. The remaining sawing and planing required is then left to the individual carpenter to undertake on site by hand. The availability of regular sawn roofing battens and rafters has enabled tiled roofs to be far more easily constructed than when only poles were available. Treatment of building timbers against termite attack has allowed these secondary hardwood species to be used for more permanent dwellings. However, many of the chemicals used are highly toxic, some being banned in Europe. Use of these chemicals should be avoided and either alternatives to timber or safer treatments should be found.

Alongside the increased use of sawn secondary hardwoods, there has been a renewed interest in the use of round poles for more permanent long-span structures. In the Imatong mountains of Southern Sudan, where there are no powered saw-mills, teak has been force-grown by close-planting (as with pine forests). After four or five years the young trees are up to six metres

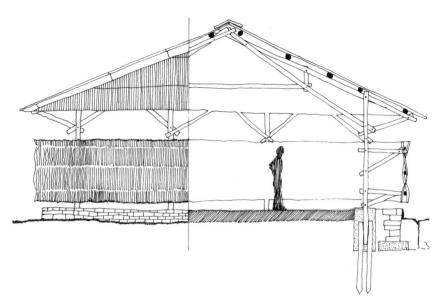

Figure 17. *Section through brickmaking shed built of round pole timber, Southern Sudan, 1976.*

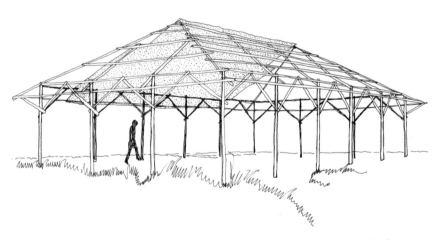

Figure 18. *Brickmaking shed constructed of round pole timber, Juba, Southern Sudan, 1976.*

long, straight and very strong as their grain is not cut. Using steel bolts for connections, large sheds have been constructed using these poles which, being teak, are highly resistant to termites.

In order to make better use of the palmwood and eucalyptus poles available to them for a school-building project in Mali, the Building Technology

43

Group at the Delft Technology University developed a hand-operated wire-lacing tool. This reduced the cost and increased the speed of making connections in these materials. With pole-timber roofs, either steeply-pitched traditional thatch or, at lower pitches, corrugated sheetmetal is appropriate.

Timber is, however, a prime example of the demand for building materials being in conflict with the need to conserve dwindling natural resources. The destruction of tropical rain forests in Brazil and elsewhere, often to produce high-quality hardwoods for export to the West, has provoked worldwide concern. For this reason, conservation-conscious builders and their clients now avoid the use of new tropical hardwoods and have switched to forest products which are farmed in a sustainable manner.

In those parts of the world where timber products are a dwindling resource, their loss perhaps contributing to desertification as in the Sahel, old building traditions are becoming obsolete and alternatives to timber need to be found. There is growing concern over this and the related issue of energy-conscious design which has influenced the formation of the so-called green architecture movement.

### Social and cultural factors

Social and cultural factors are usually the last to be considered by designers and builders. If they are from the society for which they are building, they know what is expected culturally from the building, perhaps without even needing to articulate these requirements. If they are from outside the community, builders usually concentrate on how to provide thermal comfort using local materials. They seldom attempt to understand the aspirations of the people for whom they are building, let alone how this might be translated into built form. Ive (1985) has shown that government-sponsored research in Africa

> has been overwhelmingly concentrated upon technical rather than socio-economic aspects of construction, with an emphasis in each case on the development of new materials (to substitute for more expensive or imported ones) and of new construction technologies . . . multi-lateral agencies have been highly influential in setting this research agenda.

He goes on to suggest that the dissemination of these improved technologies is limited by cultural factors. These include the low status of these new materials and products in the eyes of the affluent, and the reluctance of the poor to experiment with new materials in self-build. In Ghana experiments by Kumasi University with stabilized earth blocks were at first badly received in urban areas, despite their economic advantage over sandcrete blocks. The stabilized earth blocks were regarded as rural or 'bush' by the new urban migrants. This was because rural houses were also made from red lateritic soil and urban houses were expected to have the visual attributes of concrete, which was considered the only really modern urban material. When

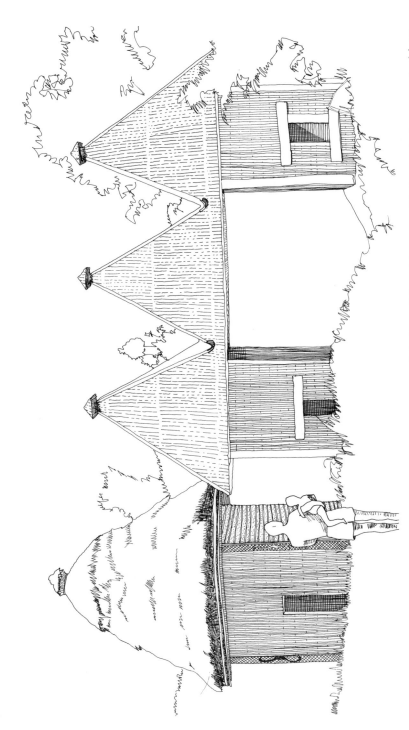

Figure 19. Thatched traditional house alongside a modified traditional house with imported corrugated iron roofs, Cameroon 1988. Note that the new roofs have been constructed, despite the extra cost, to match the shape of the older roof.

the walls were plastered and painted white then this supposedly improved form of walling was accepted for urban dwellings.

In Kenya, however the colour red had the opposite significance when assessing the status of micro-concrete tiles. As micro-concrete tiles needed to compete in both quality and price with burnt clay tiles which were red, then the introduction of pigment to the concrete mix increased their status in the eyes of the building owner. Figure 19 is another example of status overriding cost in the choice of roofing material, this time in the forest region of Cameroon. Here a steeply-pitched, thatched, traditional house is shown alongside a modified traditional house with a corrugated iron roof. The new roof is far more expensive than the almost flat roof which function demands, but status requires the steeper traditional pitch.

Societies and cultures have always had relations with one another for the purposes of trade and commerce. Different links have been forged at different times in history. Pioneering exploration led to colonialism. And since independence whole populations have moved to the cities, and graduates from developing countries have been trained in Russia and the West. Along these pathways of trade and exploration, travel not only material goods but ideas, aspirations and religions.

Such cultural ideas can have an impact on built form far more profound than any technical innovation. When the anti-French, but non-aggressive,

Figure 20. *The earth mosque at Mopti, Mali 1971.*

46

Moslem Brotherhoods increased their proselytizing over the plains of Mali in the late-nineteenth century, small mosques were built in many villages — even in the strongly animist Dogon villages mentioned earlier. Here, many of the elements of the traditional Dogon house were adapted and incorporated in the new mosque designs. The chequerboard patterns of the Dogon mother house were used for mosque walls. And the method of lighting the sanctuary was adapted from the domestic Dogon chimney form (Bourdier 1991). The impact of global culture is now so profound, however, that there is seldom time for such adaptations. Regional cultures are being rapidly transformed in ways which are only half understood.

King (1984) has shown how evocative and easily adapted to widely different aspirations a single house form can be. The bungalow, a type used in pre-colonial India, mostly as a hunting lodge for the Indian aristocracy, was adopted by the British. It became their colonial model house-type, not only for India but throughout the empire. The name was derived from the original Hindi or Mahratti *bangli*, meaning of, or belonging to, Bengal. The form proved so popular that pre-fabricated steel bungalows were shipped out to Nigeria for the use of colonial administrators. It was even adopted during

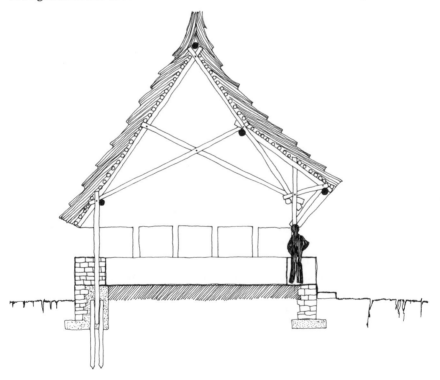

Figure 21. *Section through house built of round pole timber, stone and thatch, Juba, Southern Sudan, 1976.*

Figure 22. *House constructed of round pole timber, thatch and stone, Juba, Southern Sudan, 1976.*

the 1930s in England by workers escaping from the city to build a single-storey holiday home. Many aspired to retire to their bungalow in the country (Hardy and Ward 1984).

The direction of flow of cultural artefacts is usually less even-handed however. Said (1985) claims that European culture was able to manage, and even produce, a concept called the Orient which it came to dominate politically, sociologically, militarily, ideologically and scientifically during the post-enlightenment period. Cultural and ideological norms are seen as travelling on the back of technological innovation. As reinforced concrete was invented in Europe, so European culture is embodied in the reinforced-concrete forms imported into developing countries. Whatever the truth of such claims, it is clear that industrialization and rapid urbanization, boosted by political independence, together with the development of transportation and information systems, have had a far-reaching effect on regional cultures.

Various trends have been identified. With increased mobility and urbanization, extended family-support structures have tended to break down into nuclear families. Courtyard houses, which used to be occupied by one large family, are now inhabited by several co-tenants. Figures 23 and 24 showing two courtyard houses measured in 1972 in Ashaiman, a shanty town on the edge of the port/city of Tema in Ghana, are successive examples of this process (Mitchell 1975).

The courtyard-house plan in Figure 23 belonged to a man who settled in about 1930. Until 1960 he was a farmer. He and his immediate family, comprising his three wives, their sisters and children, occupied those rooms built of unstabilized earth facing into the courtyard. Adult male members of his extended family were accommodated in the three earth-walled rooms

48

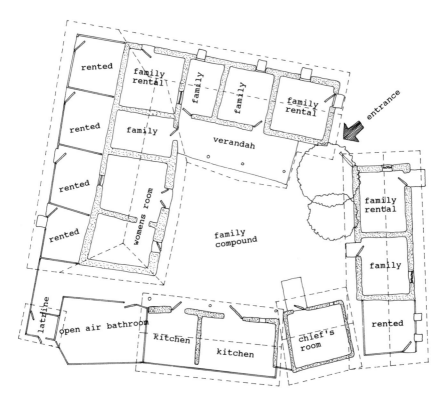

Figure 23. *The farmer's house: extended family accommodation with some recently added lean-to general rental rooms attached in Ashaiman, Ghana, 1974.*

entered from the outside of the compound. In 1960, with the new settlement pushing up against his cattle-grazing land, he changed his job to that of landlord. First, he built five lean-to rooms of packing-cases and corrugated iron against the back walls of his compound, and rented each to a different migrant family of his own tribe. Later, as the pressure for shelter increased, he constructed several timber dwellings near by, and let them out to all-comers. At the time of the survey, in 1972, he was one of the oldest and most respected members of the community.

Figure 24 is the plan of a house owned by a locksmith who came to Tema in 1958. He was about 35 years old in 1972. With money borrowed from his family in his home town, augmented by his wife's earnings as a grocer, he leased the plot and built the first part of his house. This consisted of three rooms in an L-shaped block. He let these out to three young families who had moved to the city to work in the new industrial sector. Meanwhile, he and his wife stayed with his wife's family elsewhere in Ashaiman. With his

49

rent income and more savings he built another L-shaped block, again consisting of three rooms. This time he only rented off two of these rooms as he and his wife moved into the other. Only then did they have children. In 1970 he was able to complete the courtyard house with a four-roomed rental block. By in-filling the space between the last two developments, he created for himself and his family an apartment comprising bedroom, living-room, store, small living-room and bathroom. The courtyard acts as a kitchen and general meeting-ground for all the families occupying rooms opening on to it. Outside the house, a carpenter rents the space under a tree as his workshop and the owner's wife runs a grocery kiosk near by. The wives of the tenants sell sweets, soap and charcoal to passers-by on the street.

Duncan (1982) calls this process individualization. With urbanization and increased exposure to a cash economy in a more open society, traditional hierarchical family structures loosen and the individual is encouraged to make ties outside his immediate kinship group. In the examples illustrated, both courtyard houses which have been progressively adapted over the last half-century to cope with the increasing demand for space, the process of individualization has produced a change in the socio-cultural use of space.

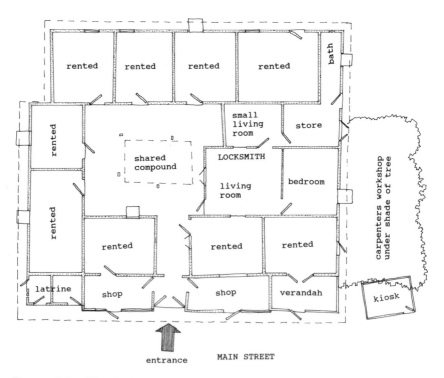

Figure 24. *The locksmith's house: rental accommodation for nuclear families in a courtyard house in Ashaiman, Ghana, 1974.*

50

This is quite apart from the change from unstabilized earth walls to packing-case frames in the farmer's house, and to a concrete block structure for the locksmith's house.

Strangely, new settlements can also generate more, rather than less, clearly defined spatial separations. Bilbeisi (1990) has shown that when Bedouin nomads have been settled by the Jordanian government in newly-constructed villages, many of the traditions of hospitality associated with the black tent are loosened. Privacy is more clearly articulated, using high walls and separate entrances. Religion plays a more important role in imposing codes of behaviour on next-door neighbours, who can no longer simply move off at the first sign of a dispute.

Pellow (1988) has shown however, that in a multi-cultural, rapidly expanding urban context, privacy and social segregation is adjusted to take account of the need for easier social exchange. Sabon Zongo is a Hausa community which was established in 1912 in Accra, Ghana. Originally, houses were built with an entry hut for the use of the house-owner and his male friends. Women's quarters were segregated and sheltered from the view of unrelated males. By the 1980s however, houses had been adapted and new houses built without these features. After independence in 1957, and the rapid growth in the population of the capital city associated with increased industrialization, it became more difficult for discrete communities within the city fabric to remain quite so isolated. As a result their house form has been adapted accordingly. Pellow argues that 'one sees the conflation of Hausa vernacular, southern Ghanaian traditions and western influence'.

Another trend within Ghanaian society, which is related to the development of house form, has been identified by Ongom (1990). He argues that increased education has not only encouraged the drift to the towns where work requiring academic skills may be found, but also influenced changes in social structure. Western-educated elites, such as doctors, lawyers, teachers and businessmen, replaced the upper echelon of traditional society and introduced many of the values of their British teachers. They were expected to convert to Christianity. The elites were therefore monogamous and their houses were smaller than polygamous households. Houses provided by the government for their civil servants were detached single-storey houses where the parents slept separately from their children. Each room in these houses was allocated to a specific activity — cooking in the kitchen, eating in the dining-room, receiving guests and story-telling in the living-room. Previously, in a traditional house, all these, as well as other activities, would have taken place in the courtyard.

Ongom states that one of the chief characteristics of these elites is their imitability. Their values and aspirations filter down to the rest of the population. Figure 25 is a drawing done by a young secondary-school leaver in 1974 when asked to illustrate how he would like to live. It shows himself as John Wayne walking the streets of Accra where the houses are

51

Figure 25. *'John Wayne patrolling the streets of Accra'. A drawing by a Ghanaian schoolboy, 1974.*

three-storey, flat-roofed, air-conditioned, concrete-framed blocks, with televisions and flying the national flag. Even the anti-burglar grilles over the windows have acquired status.

Better educational opportunities and the freeing of gender roles have allowed women to play an increasingly powerful role in those spheres of life traditionally forbidden. In addition to the change from extended to nuclear families, there has been a rapid increase in the number of households headed by women. In the urban areas of Latin America and Africa, this figure can exceed fifty per cent (Moser and Peake 1987). In such a changing situation women, who have had ample experience of working without such services as water supply, sanitation and serviced cooking facilities, are often in the best position to make decisions about the ordering of priorities for upgrading such services, in adaptations to house design and in the planning of community facilities.

The locksmith's house shown in Figure 24 is an example of how, when space is at a premium, there is often a need to supplement family income by operating a small business or craft activity in part of the house. Often it is the women who control the household budget and who will most easily manage the home-located business.

## Economy

Most of the changes discussed so far relate to moves towards an urban cash economy. Ever since the industrial revolution in Europe, cities have ex-anded rapidly. Even New York has had its period of shanty settlements. In the developing world, urbanization has accelerated with independence from colonial rule.

In an urban shanty town everything, including much which in a rural situation would be taken for granted, has a cash value. Space is at a premium. Earth for building cannot be taken from any site without leaving a dangerous borrow-pit. It must be shipped in from a quarry instead. There is no surrounding forest from which to cut timber, and this ceases to be cheap. Even the paper packaging of cement bags has a value as wrapping-paper for market food. There is little or no time for building your own house, unless you have the skills to do it faster and cheaper than those who do it every day. There is increased skill specialization. This is because you can earn more cash working at your speciality in order to pay a builder than you can save by doing it yourself. In such a situation the pace of city life does not welcome materials for construction which are anything but the most durable that can be afforded. The search is for low-cost permanent building materials and maintenance-free durable housing.

The first shack erected on an urban plot may very well be temporary — perhaps even erected overnight by its inhabitants. From then on however, if successful, the family will replace and adapt this replacement with a staged permanent development. Urban settlements which were squatter areas can turn into prosperous neighbourhoods in less than a generation. The Zabbaleen community living in Manshiet Nasser in Cairo, which thrives on the collection and recycling of rubbish, has transformed its housing stock over the past five years:

In many of the houses the squealing of pigs competes with the din of electric motors [of the waste-recycling machines]. Where there were once

53

shacks thrown together with corrugated iron and chipped rock, there are now three- or four-storey brick houses.

(Bouverie 1991)

Materials and labour skills have a cash value. And so do goods and services, buildings and land. Obtaining title to the plot of land on which he or she has first squatted is of major concern to the city-dweller. Compare this to the traditional Hausa view of land described in the last section where value was placed solely on its current use.

It is not only a question of owning sufficient land to build a house but also of proximity to work, water, schools and shops; that is, a question of location. Fire hazards, water supply, waste disposal, sanitation and noise pollution may be absent or easily dealt with in a rural environment. In the city, they must be faced on a low income. This is where government tries to provide services and address these issues by land provision and serviced-plot allocation, banks and building societies to provide loans — but only for permanent houses which are an appreciating asset — building standards to assure building quality adequate to secure a loan, roads and sewers, water supply and drainage, electric light and power. However, government is under-resourced for this task and raising outside finance from international donors is difficult. Banks cannot lend a sum to individuals without a secure job, as it is unlikely to be repaid. Building codes often set unreachable quality standards and their enforcement becomes, at best, impossible and, at worst, destructive. The provision of other services is sporadic.

These problems do not stop the flood of city migrants, and new grass-roots structures have emerged to begin to cope with these problems. Well located but hitherto unusable land on the edge of cities is regularly squatted (Ward 1982). Invasions of land are carefully organized by the squatters themselves and may be carried out over a period of a few days (UNCHS 1982). Title is often obtained after prolonged political action by squatters' groups. In West Africa traditional *susu* savings societies, which were originally used by market women to save to start up in business, have been adapted for house savings (Little 1970). Illegal connections to mains water supplies, night soil collection, road repair and even plans for future development are often provided by the community itself without direct recourse to authority.

This section of chapter two has briefly laid out the effects which urbanization and the change to a cash economy are having on the relationship between built form and context. What is the appropriate role for government in such a situation? The relevance of grass-roots community initiative within the context of a prevailing lack of government finance is examined next.

## THE ROLE OF GOVERNMENT IN SHELTER PROVISION

People still build houses for themselves in shanty towns, just as they did traditionally in the countryside. This is despite the changes associated with industrialization, urbanization, independence and modernization. Turner (1976) argues that there is a universal need to house oneself — a process which is in itself a cultural expression of individual identity. Burgess (1978), however, is a notable critic of this approach. He argues that people are encouraged to house themselves in order that the government may avoid its responsibility for housing the population.

Whether or not the governments of developing countries should build low-income housing for their populations, it is clear that they are unable to do so adequately for lack of resources. The self-help process will ensure that low-income urban migrants continue to construct shelters in accordance with the resources available to them and with their aspirations for a better life, for the forseeable future.

However, governments do recognize that they have some responsibility to provide for low-income settlement. At Habitat, the Conference on Human Settlement called by the United Nations in 1976 in Vancouver, 136 nations approved 64 Recommendations for National Action; these included:

○ The need for each nation to establish a comprehensive national settlements policy linked to socio-economic development policy
○ Increased public control of land use
○ Increased support for the construction sector (including the informal sector)
○ Priority to the provision of safe drinking water and hygienic disposal of household and human wastes for the whole population, and
○ New institutions at 'national, ministerial and other appropriate levels of government' to formulate and implement the policy with public participation as an indispensable element.

(Hardoy and Satterthwaite 1982)

Writing in 1981, having surveyed 17 developing countries who were signatories to the Habitat recommendations, Hardoy and Satterthwaite concluded that a squatter's shack was still a more appropriate response to the needs of the urban poor than heavily subsidized public housing. The government's efforts and limited resources were better aimed elsewhere. They emphasized the following areas where governments could have a real effect:

○ The provision of adequately serviced supplies of land suitably located for low-income housing. The first requirement would be a legislative frame-work for land acquisition. This is because the urban poor can pay little or nothing for the security of tenure required by the squatter to give him or her the confidence with which to begin the phased construction of a permanent dwelling. It also requires the supply of roads, water, electricity and sewerage to a standard appropriate to the resources available and the size of the population to be served. Site-and-service schemes, which have been proposed by national governments and supported by the United Nations and the World Bank, are based on this concept

- The revision of building standards to encourage better-quality construction. But not to demand unrealistically what is desirable when the local building industry is unable to attain such standards and the population cannot afford them
- The support of local building-materials industries in their efforts to expand and develop more permanent indigenous materials. This could be encouraged through the funding of local research stations and the examination of codes which encouraged the use of local materials
- The collection and dissemination of relevant data — on demography, the state of the building industry, and on existing settlement provision, for instance. This is to assess the changes that are taking place, so that resources can be properly allocated, and
- The provision of training schemes at all levels of the process of housing. This would ensure that the skills required were available both within the government infrastructure and the local population.

A clear way forward, seen as a partnership between the self-help urban squatter on the one hand and the national government on the other, could now be discerned. If we can agree with Turner that the value of a house is not only based on its market value — that it is not a product that should be provided to everyone as of right, that it is a much more independent process of saving, building, maintaining and improving, and that it is a medium for cultural change and expression — then we can accept the limitation of government's role to the servicing of the self-help constructor. But governments have taken a wide variety of attitudes to such a definition of roles. Salas (1988) documented five types of response displayed by Latin American governments in the 1980s towards the phenomenon of auto-construction or self-help. These ranged from the policy of hostility in Venezuela where the government of Perez Jimenez declared 'war on the rancho' through policies of indifference and toleration to those of sponsorship and promotion in Mexico.

The situation was highlighted when the United Nations declared 1987 International Year of Shelter for the Homeless (IYSH). It was aimed at pavement dwellers, those made homeless by disasters, and those without a real home. A real home was defined as shelter providing protection from the elements, with water and other services, security of tenure, and safety. Projects were initiated and funded by the international community through national governments and non-government organizations (NGOs). Summing up the previous decade for the United Nations Centre for Human Settlements, Rodwin (1987) stated that in many countries the decision-making power was concentrated at the top level of government. And that lack of consultation

56

with users was having an adverse effect on population distribution, settlement patterns, shelter and servicing.

The task ahead therefore seems to be one of finding effective ways for government and self-help owner-builders to participate in providing a steadily improving quality and permanence of product, while at the same time allowing self-builders to reach for their increasingly individualistic goals.

From the government's side, training, building standards and subsidy are the tools employed, often in an integrated programme. Training and subsidy are offered in return for compliance with building standards. Such self-help programmes absorb discontent and enhance government legitimacy. Subsidy of housing emphasizes the government's public responsibility and allows standards to be introduced incrementally, whilst maintaining some measure of local control. Salas (1988) states that a plurality of such self-help schemes is required if they are to have any chance of solving the housing problem. Diversity would depend on the aims of the people and the response of government. Such schemes might involve varying degrees of government training and credit arrangements, together with a mix of external and local management and funding, building-material supply and tool-sharing.

On the other hand, from the building owner's point of view, self-help is often more important as a rallying-point for threatened sections of the population than as a means of cheapening housing by the use of free labour (Schuman 1986). The concerted action of the residents is first used to demand security of tenure. It is then organized to construct shelter against the odds, which include the inertia of government bureaucracy. In an urban economy, financial institutions regard a house as a commodity, whose value is determined by what it can fetch in the market-place. In such a situation, self-help can temporarily decommodify the process. This gives dignity to the task and appropriates the product for the self-builder who is empowered to use the building process as an expression of his or her aspirations.

Birch (1981) describes a sites-and-services programme in Somalia aimed at settling nomads. Here, a training programme was successfully introduced to control the quality of construction. One construction adviser, doubling as a building-control officer, was provided for every 50 building workers. These advisers were government employees, skilled in building trades, who provided on-the-job training. This was found to be more effective than formal training courses in this case. In other schemes, however, with larger, faster-growing communities, training and technical assistance was given directly to local builders and building-material suppliers. Here, there was greater specialization of labour and this more focused training was seen as a long-term investment in higher-quality construction.

Initiated in the early 1970s, the Tema Co-operative Housing scheme (Mitchell 1975) is an example of training providing a two-way bridge between government and grass-roots organizations. The Ghanaian government had previously been used to providing public housing through the Tema Development Corporation, using public funds from the Bank for Housing and Construction, with the State Construction Corporation carrying out the work.

A pilot project was initiated by Kumasi University for a core housing scheme on the edge of the shanty town of Ashaiman. A social survey had established the existence of local *susu* savings organizations which were used by the urban newcomers to save the capital required to set up a small market stall for example. Alternative funding arrangements were also needed to provide housing. Building on the results of the social survey a credit union was formed, aimed at providing funds for its members who would occupy the houses produced. The university team became a technical service organization, which formed a link between the large government organizations listed above and their parallel local organizations formed during the course of the project.

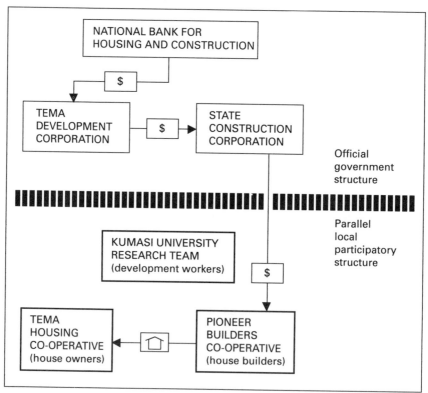

Figure 26. *Diagram showing how the embryo local grass roots co-operative structure developing in parallel with the official structure first received house building finance from the Ghanaian Government (1970).*

The Tema Housing Co-operative (the house-owners and local client) convinced the Bank for Housing and Construction of its ability to keep accounts and collect regular payments from its members through its operation as a credit union. It was then authorized to receive a low-interest loan through the Tema Development Corporation. The local Pioneer Builders Co-operative, made up of tradesmen trained during the course of the project, subcontracted the whole of the work from the State Construction Corporation.

Once this first scheme proved successful, the National Co-operative Council took on the responsibility for housing co-operatives within a legislative framework provided by government. This framework provided for the registration of local co-operatives, their training by the Technical Service Organization, and their eligibility for subsidy with a low-interest revolving loan for house construction.

From information received in February 1992 it was clear that 22 years after its inception, the Tema Housing Co-operative was still operating successfully. The small revolving fund continued to produce houses despite

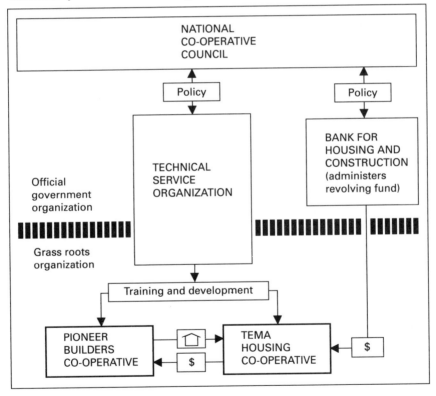

Figure 27. *Diagram showing the developed co-operative housing structure linking official with grass roots organizations.*

a massive devaluation of the Ghanaian currency. The original 21 houses had been increased to 106 and the co-operative had been allocated further land by the Tema Development Corporation to build more core houses. Some co-operative members had been able to repay their loans and owned their house within the co-operative structure. Maintenance was budgeted for within the monthly payments of workers. Elections to the management committee were held yearly and the accounts of the co-operative were audited regularly by the National Co-operative Council.

Some of the key elements of the success of the Tema project are echoed in the experience described in chapter four. A close and lengthy involvement with the local community resulted in the formation of a credit union in Tema. In Muka Mukuu building work was preceded by social surveys and communication work which helped establish local building committees where project priorities could be discussed. On the other hand in Zambia progress on the school building programme was slow because of the villagers' lack of interest. Their involvement had not been sought at an early stage, nor had they been adequately consulted. The development of grass-roots participatory structures in parallel with official government organizations was a hallmark of Tema's success. Development workers working in Bhutan on the national school-building programme have since 1986 sought energetically to move away from the headquarters of the project at Thimphu closer to field work with the local community. Still under the auspices of the school-building programme, workers have been posted to remote site supervisor posts where contact with users of the schools and their parents has been more direct. This has led to their involvement with parents in constructing 'extended classrooms' or 'community schools'.

### The building-materials industry

As we have seen in the previous section, another major role played by government is that of support to the local building-materials industry. Housing is often a low priority on the list of projects for the use of imported materials such as cement and cementitious products. Governments are therefore seeking to develop local alternatives to this material. Similarly, local materials such as timber can be developed into new building products such as plywood. Unfortunately, when allocating resources, governments and international organizations often divide the building and building-materials industries of developing countries into formal and informal sectors.

The informal sector is characterized by some or all of the following attributes:

○ Construction is carried out by the occupier or his family with a minimal cash cost
○ Buildings have a high maintenance cost and a short life
○ Building codes and standards are ignored and irrelevant

o There is a high degree of uncertainty as to the title of the land on which the building is erected
o Whilst an occupier may incur a debt in kind to other members of his extended family or home village for the labour and materials used in construction, no cash mortgage is raised from any lending institution, and
o There is no professional involvement.

The prime consideration in the informal sector is to build using as little cash as possible.
The formal sector on the other hand:

o Uses cash, borrowed from a bank or other lending institution
o Employs trades people, contractors, professionals
o Constructs a building with a low maintenance cost and long life
o Builds on land where there is a clear legal agreement with the owner
o Builds to standards and codes of practice laid down by statute, and
o Produces a building which has high long-term value in the sense that it is a mortgageable asset.

When considering investing in the formal sector, a bank will compare the value of the building with the cost of investment.

The use of local materials in the informal sector is not only appropriate but extensive. However, their adoption for use within the formal sector has met with resistance from local, national and international authorities, lending institutions, and occupiers. The reasons for this resistance can be summarized as a lack of confidence in the fitness for purpose of these materials in terms of:

o Physical properties (for example strength, durability, fire-resistance) and therefore the perceived maintenance cost and life of the building
o Safety and public health, and
o Looks and style, as a symbol of the perceived aims of the occupier.

This has led to banks and lending institutions having little confidence in the value of the product and therefore being reluctant to lend funds for building with local materials.

In addition, governments often seek to avoid responsibility, in terms of service and welfare provision and in cases of disaster, for large sections of the urban population who squat without title on marginal land and construct their dwellings within the informal sector without complying with government standards.

Drewer (1982) suggests that housing is more likely to involve the informal than the formal sector of the economy. He suggests moreover that these sectors operate with totally different materials-supply, and financial and

61

contractual mechanisms. The informal sector is employed 'because of price advantages, undisclosed subsidies implicit in the nature of the informal sector or a wish to avoid bringing the building under formal controls'.

Introducing new or improved local materials is therefore difficult as we are faced with a catch-22 situation. Residents with very limited resources are reluctant to experiment with new materials or to give up the other advantages of operating in the informal sector. On the other hand, the employment of testing and quality-control procedures, leading to improved standards, is essential to the success of government in both developing and promoting such materials.

In order to examine the role played by standards and quality-control procedures in the development of the building-materials industry, we have set out below the case of the introduction of Portland cement to the United Kingdom building-materials industry in the late-nineteenth century. We have then compared this with its recent introduction as an earth-block stabilizer in developing countries.

## The introduction of Portland cement

On 21 October 1824 the inventor of Portland cement, Joseph Aspdin, was granted a patent for his product. However, it was not until 1860 that its use became widespread. That was the year that John Grant, assistant engineer to London's Metropolitan Board of Works, established a regular and formalized testing service for a variety of cements. It was as a consequence of the introduction of tests that there was a general improvement in the strength of Portland cement in 1863. The delay of nearly 40 years in the widespread adoption of this revolutionary material can be attributed to the lack of confidence in the material and its various imitations, which only the establishment of independent testing procedures allayed (Francis 1977). Once the larger cement companies realized the importance of high standards in the marketing of their product, in-house testing laboratories and quality-control measures were established in most factories.

## The production of soil-cement blocks

Quality control is clearly easier in a controlled factory situation than on site. Thus factory-based block manufacture is more likely to be of a consistently high quality than on-site production. Whereas codes of practice can be written for on-site manufacture, the only guarantee of quality is to test the finished product. To date, most of the machines for earth-block manufacture have been designed to be used on rural sites where earth is freely available. The site production of strong, weather-resistant blocks has been a hit-and-miss affair. In stabilizing earth, it is not only the finished block which must be tested. Where no graded quarry material is available, the soil, which can vary in its consistency from site to site, and even within the same site, must be tested to check its suitability as a raw material for block production.

Comparing the production of earth blocks on site with that of concrete blocks in a factory, we might reasonably suppose that the lack of quality associated with stabilized earth blocks is due to the on-site nature of the production process rather than the theoretical capacity of the soil for stabilization.

Even sand and aggregate quarries in developed countries test and grade their products before sale. Soil for block production is quarried on site and must be tested by unskilled labour with rudimentary techniques. Yet, if stabilized soil is to be accepted within the formal sector, it must be suitable for use in urban areas. The difficulty is that, in urban areas, these on-site techniques have none of the advantages associated with rural production (such as free raw material and no transport costs) but all the disadvantages associated with poor quality control.

Clearly, the assurance of fitness-for-purpose offered by building standards and codes of practice for a newly-improved local material can generate confidence leading to its acceptance within the formal sector. So, the role of standards and codes of practice within a developing economy can be used not only to protect public health and safety, but also to set a standard of quality which could encourage the development of valuable products from within the local economy.

Although, in theory, standards could have this effect, unfortunately they seldom do. Lloyd (1986) has shown that in countries which have recently become independent, building standards and codes are modelled on, or may even be direct copies of, those used by the ex-colonial European power or the USA. These standards take little or no account of local conditions such as:

o The availability of local resources
o Climate
o The current state of the local economy, and
o The current pressures on the building industry (for example, urban housing crisis, scarcity of imported materials, transport and distribution difficulties in rural areas, lack of necessary building skills, techniques or plant).

In Saudi Arabia, urban zoning regulations were prepared by American consultants whose vision was of a detached prairie house looking outwards over its own stretch of land. The Saudi Arabian reality is quite different however. On relatively small urban plots, the buildings were required to be set back by two metres from the boundary in order to limit fire spread from plot to plot and to guarantee adequate lighting and ventilation. On plots of only 20 metres by 20 metres this regulation ensured that all buildings had to be detached island buildings.

Saudi Arabia and other Gulf countries have a well established tradition of

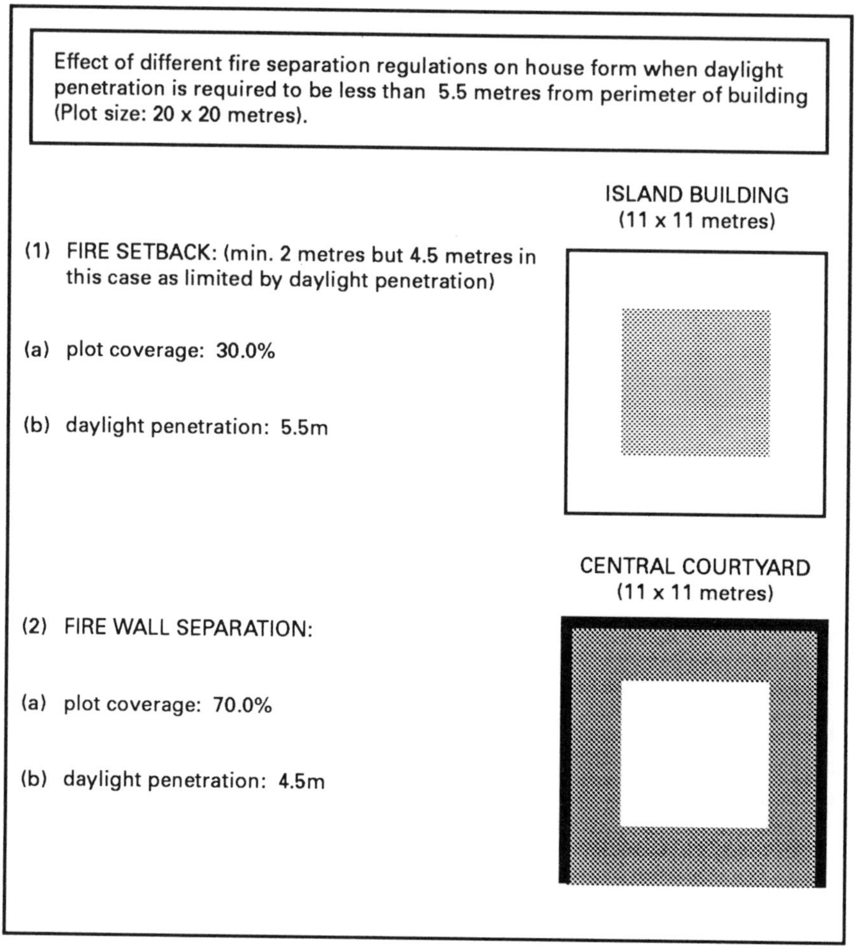

ISLAND BUILDING
(11 x 11 metres)

(1) FIRE SETBACK: (min. 2 metres but 4.5 metres in this case as limited by daylight penetration)

(a) plot coverage: 30.0%

(b) daylight penetration: 5.5m

CENTRAL COURTYARD
(11 x 11 metres)

(2) FIRE WALL SEPARATION:

(a) plot coverage: 70.0%

(b) daylight penetration: 4.5m

Figure 28. *Diagram of the effect of building regulations on house form in Saudi Arabia (after Lloyd).*

urban building based on the courtyard house which performs well in terms of climate and privacy. Privacy is a factor which is of overwhelming concern in this Islamic state. The island buildings were denied privacy through being overlooked. They also needed to be air-conditioned for comfort, unlike their courtyard alternative. Formal studies later showed that using a central courtyard could obtain greater densities whilst ensuring the same qualities of daylight and ventilation. Fire separation was obtained by specifying that the boundary wall should resist the passage of fire for two hours. The regulations were subsequently changed from the rigid set-back rules to a more sophisticated plot-ratio system which allowed the Saudis to build either type of dwelling.

Similarly a case study of low-cost housing for the Fijian Housing Authority in Chapter Four confirms the inappropriateness of building standards and planning regulations invented for use in the UK and New Zealand for the culture and economic conditions of the capital, Suva.

Greenstreet (1983) has demonstrated that the experience of the developed world has been that breakthroughs in technology leap ahead of the legalistic frameworks of building control. Traditionally, the customs of the trade concerned were sufficient to monitor the effects of new buildings on health and safety. However, with rapid urbanization and its accompanying technological change, legislative provision for public protection from such increased hazards as fire spread and disease carried by insanitary conditions were required. Control provisions can be either:

o Specific requirements categorically stating the materials and construction required
o Functional requirements which state only the detailed capacity of the construction to have, for example, a safety factor of twice the maximum likely load imposed, or limit the passage of fire for one hour, and
o Performance requirements which are much looser and more open to different interpretation and might only state, for example, that there shall be an adequate factor of safety when calculating loading, and adequate time for the occupants to escape in case of fire.

In countries where building control is rudimentary, the requirements tend to be specific, needing minimum interpretation. Such controls are anti-innovatory, protective of established practices and anti-entrepreneurial. They certainly do not encourage the introduction of new improved local materials into the formal sector.

In recognition of the role in confidence-building which the testing of new and improved materials can play, governments have established Building Research Centres (Building Research Establishment 1980). However, these centres are usually under-funded and, as we have seen, have often inherited inappropriate building codes. In the developed countries, private materials industries have established trade associations particular to specific materials (such as the Cement and Concrete Association in the United Kingdom). These aim to set confidence-boosting international standards. Developing countries, on the other hand, do not have the resources to fund their own market-led research into specific materials. Nevertheless, in the formal sector, contractors are required to fulfil standards set internationally. It is not surprising, therefore, that the adoption of local materials from the informal to the formal sector, and their improvement, is inhibited.

**The role of the professional development worker**

In this complex trade-off of responsibility for shelter provision between government and people, what role should the professional development worker play? To understand the role he or she is able to play it is useful to look back at the history of professionalism, how this particular form of specialization came about and the different roles it has played in times of change and development. A criticism of previous professional practice will help to contribute to the sound and informed choice of roles by future development workers.

We are concerned with the process of building and we have shown that this process is subject to constant change. The building skills in the formal sector are more specialized, the trades involved more clearly differentiated, than in either the traditional or informal sectors. The development of a separate category of building worker called professional, whether architect, engineer or surveyor, is a relatively recent phenomenon in western society:

> Even in the mid-eighteenth century, architecture in Britain could not be described as distinct from the rest of the building process. Nor was there any sense in which the practice was limited to an exclusive group of specially trained people . . . Yet within a period of not much more than a century, not only was a significant proportion of design work to become entirely removed from the process of construction, but also architectural practice was to be confined to a group of men who specialized in the design of buildings and who occupied a position independent of both client and builders.
>
> Forty undated

This is the situation in the formal sector. Generally, the professional's role is one of producing drawings, describing the client's requirements to the builder, and ensuring that these requirements are carried out. In traditional societies, as we have seen in the case of the Draa valley in Morocco, this responsibility was vested in the skilled building worker. However, no drawings were required as there were plenty of examples of similar houses already existing to illustrate the builder's proposals to the client. In preliterate societies, there were no professionals as such — designs were copied from previous examples, and innovation was by trial and error.

Turner describes the formal sector, with specialized building trades and professions, as a closed system. The user (house-occupier) is differentiated from the client (government agency). The needs of the user are often quite distinct from the requirements of the client, and yet the user is not consulted.

Building workers have often defined such clear roles for themselves that important areas fall outside anyone's remit, rather like the demarcation disputes we have seen in the West. For example, as primary health-care has been classified within the remit of the medical profession, provision for suitable water-supply, sanitary and waste systems have sometimes been given low priority. Architects and planners define their role as being concerned with built form and its use. Doctors tend to concentrate on clinical remedy or prevention. As Hardoy and Satterthwaite (1987) write:

non-medical activities such as community water supply are rejected as less cost-effective than medical interventions such as oral rehydration therapy (ORT) for diarrhoea in children . . . ORT has led to great improvement in the treatment of child diarrhoea. But its long-term impacts can be but limited if the risks of contracting diarrhoea again through contaminated water . . . are not addressed.

Criticism of the role of professionals in this closed system was articulated by Ivan Illich (1977). He characterized the professions in the West, at that time, as disabling. Professional elites defined problems which people were supposed to have, and then determined solutions which were applied to them. As a response, primarily to the criticisms inherent in Illich's work, some professionals began to describe themselves as enablers. They would work in an open system to provide the materials and skills necessary for the users to solve their own problems, as defined by themselves.

According to Turner (1984), the key difference between an enabling and a disabling professional is in their attitude to knowledge. The enabler is primarily a sharer of knowledge. 'Learning should be a conscious part of all activities and when the professional is an enabler, he or she is a teacher or learner by definition,' he says.

The development worker should therefore avoid an approach which involves preconceived notions of problem or solution. For this reason, one of the most important professional skills required of a development worker is that of communication. Models, drawings and presentation techniques can help demonstrate or develop an idea, whatever its source. The development worker can use such methods to encourage the community to participate in collective action of its own choice in a coherent and pragmatic manner.

In the discussion above we have shown that, in order to enable and facilitate self-builders to realize their aspirations, community involvement, reflective participation, and a slow listening-and-learning approach are thought to be essential. This is often in conflict with the perceived wish of many fieldworkers to achieve something in the short time available to them — something of quality and permanence which adds to the cash value of the housing stock.

In many short term projects funded by national and international agencies where there is a rush to achieve results without heed to the listening process, the proposed solutions simply don't work. What is perhaps far worse than the failure of the project itself, however, is the effect on the local population. Unless failures are well explained, hope and expectations are lowered and support for trying out other ideas in the future is reduced.

Chapter Three opens with some guidelines or approaches to practical problems which may be encountered in the field. It then goes on to describe the experience of fieldworkers in a variety of projects in many parts of the world where the problems and issues of change, and its effect on traditional ways, are being tackled every day.

# PART II
*Practice*

# CHAPTER THREE
# Guidelines For Development Workers And Agencies

Whether making and repairing buckets and frying-pans with tinsmiths, or offering advice to businessmen and women through formal credit institutions, fieldworkers are involved at a wide variety of levels. Some like to work in a small, well-supported office, while others prefer to work in the field. At regional level in Bhutan, for instance, development workers have identified a need for a network of professional postings at several different levels.

But wherever and at whatever level their valuable years overseas are spent, what benefits are intended to accrue to both the aid agency and the host community? For fieldworkers, is this period primarily an educational experience? Does it contribute to their wider view of the world and other cultures? Does this allow a clearer insight into their own identity on returning home to pick up their careers where they left off? Are they only intended to 'arrive where they started, and know the place for the first time' (Edwards 1983)? Or is there, particularly in the technical fields, a role as a development worker — part of a wider professional career engaged in contributing to the process of technical change and the attendant socio-cultural ramifications, wherever these occur?

The examples recorded in this book speak for themselves. The experience is a two-way process. It is an exchange between the aid agency and the host community. What is important is that this should be a good exchange. The guidelines listed below are intended to be useful to all development workers and to their in-country colleagues. Lessons learnt from Fiji, Belize and Nepal are intended to inform the development debate in Kenya and Ghana and vice versa.

Often jobs, as defined before posting, do not turn out as expected and, faced with this situation, fieldworkers need to be flexible in their approach to their work, even to the extent that sometimes they will be expected to completely redefine their jobs. Peter Gilbert, a field director in Kenya, is quoted as saying that, in some of the most worthwhile and challenging projects, 'all you get is an identity card, the rest is up to you'. This is perhaps most likely in shorter or one-off postings where very little preparatory work has been done prior to posting. While there is no doubt that flexibility is required by fieldworkers, guideline 6 below recommends that aid agencies concentrate their resources on those projects which have been entered into after thorough feasibility studies have been carried out, where a long term commitment is entered into, and where regular assessments of progress are made. In this way greater support and direction can be given to the development worker.

These guidelines are drawn from the survey of the current debate on development work in the building field in Chapter Two, and are informed by the specific experiences detailed in Chapter Four. They are not to be considered as a checklist for all situations, but nevertheless represent a useful framework within which to analyse and assess work in this field. If they can help in the identification and evaluation of an appropriate role for aid agencies elsewhere, so much the better.

## GUIDELINES

### 1 First making contact with the user

Many fieldworkers find it difficult working in government offices without access to the end-user.

o Of particular interest was the situation in Bhutan (see p. 93). Starting in 1986, a succession of development workers worked on the national school-building programme. At first, postings were to the programme's headquarters. However, under pressure from fieldworkers to be involved with the local communities and have a training role, the next round of postings were as site-supervisors to more rural locations. Subsequently there was a move by workers in-post to move to even more remote locations where there was direct contact with the parents constructing so-called extended classrooms in their villages. Here, the upgrading of local materials and the use of Appropriate Technology was not only a way of getting the classrooms constructed but, as a building process familiar to the users, allowed easier communication during that process

o At Keroka in Kenya (see p. 92), Brian Marler was assured that the land, on which he had been asked to build the training centre, was allocated for the project. He nevertheless encountered strong objections from local farmers when the land was occupied for construction. Only when meetings had been set up with the local community, and places offered at the centre for the farmers' children, was work able to proceed. The link with the local community had been made and remained for the rest of the project

o At Muka Mukuu, Kenya (see p. 77), involvement with the local community was planned from the start. Anne Martin set up building committees at each of 10 primary-school sites. She paid particular attention to the views of women. Even so, she wished that the local community could have determined the use of the houses which were built, as she felt that this would have made this use more effective. Their designation as teachers' accommodation was predetermined. It was not until it was discovered that

71

the teachers preferred to live elsewhere and travel to the schools, that it was agreed that some of these houses could serve community functions such as clinics and group meeting-places, as well as being residential accommodation, and

○ In Fiji (see p. 111), Dave Allen, who was working as a planner setting out housing-plots for site-and-service schemes on difficult, steep, rocky land, was not given access to the future users of these sites. He was therefore obliged to represent their needs in purely financial terms in his submissions to the World Bank. Without a user-group to which he could refer, he had no criteria, other than their theoretical income grouping, to measure their socio-cultural requirements. His solution to this problem was to leave unbuilt those sections of the shelter which could be built later by their occupants.

The first guideline is therefore that a fieldworker should make contact with the users of the work which is being undertaken. Ideally they should encourage the setting up of a local committee to liaise with and advise them, and to co-ordinate activity with the local community. Fieldworkers who spend the first six months of their time concentrating on listening, and learning the views of the local community, operating a slowly, slowly approach, are more likely to produce work which is acceptable to the users.

## 2 Studying local building traditions

One of the easiest ways to begin to understand the climate, culture and technology which is immediately available, is to examine the local building traditions.

○ In Bhutan (see p. 94), Rob Fielding made a particular study of traditional architecture. This was a Buddhist culture, similar to that in Tibet. The repository of building knowledge was in the monasteries. This knowledge was not written down but was controlled by the monks.

Fieldworkers have sought to spread knowledge of local building techniques by drawings and models and in this way to have a medium for communicating with the users of their buildings.

○ Andy Bennett at Muka Mukuu, Kenya (see p. 77), spent a great deal of time listening to local builders, visiting other sites, and learning about local materials in the Muka Mukuu area before starting work himself.

A study of local building techniques and traditional building vocabularies gives the fieldworker an insight into the local building industry, and a language for communication with local building workers. A knowledge of the process of building is also a way of introducing oneself to the cultural significance of building in the area.

72

**3 Establishing a clear process of exchange and communication with the local community**

The involvement of the local community and those working on the project should be maintained throughout the project. When those working on the project are also the future users of the buildings, then the relationship with the fieldworker can be particularly fruitful.

o Muka Mukuu, Kenya (see p. 77), was originally intended to be a wholly self-help project. The largely agricultural population were assumed to be available for building work during those periods of the year when no farming work was undertaken. Unfortunately, the crop had not been very successful in previous years and families were obliged to look for cash jobs to buy food. This left little time for unpaid building work. Good communication between project staff and the local community enabled a clear food-and-training deal to be devised which was acceptable to workers on the building sites; and

o In contrast to this, at Luanshya in Zambia (see p. 103), progress in self-help school-building was poor due to lack of interest from the villagers. Nicholas Osborne described problems in this project as being mainly social rather than technical.

**4 Testing products by exposure to the real economy**

Any piece of new technology introduced to a project or developed within a project should be exposed to the market-place to discover not only its economic viability, but also the social and cultural implications of its adoption. How do people adapt the products developed within a project for use elsewhere? What are the multiplier effects of these innovations? It is important not to arrive at a project with a preconceived solution which apparently worked elsewhere, and looking for a problem to fit it. Rather, a development worker should contribute knowledge to the debate with the local community and help devise prototypes which can be assessed and developed in the context of that project. As we have discussed earlier, new technologies come loaded with the cultural baggage which have attended their previous applications. Such interventions can have effects which should not be ignored.

o In Nepal (see p. 96), Lucky Lowe was required to introduce an Indian block press which was shown to produce sound, stabilized soil-blocks. Because of the particular market conditions, this product did not compare either in price or strength and durability with fired brick, with which it would have had to compete in the type of two-storey structure for which it might have been used. This intervention was therefore abandoned.

Fibre-concrete tiling has been successfully introduced in several countries, but with different local adaptations of the original Intermediate Technology Development Group (ITDG) design.

- In Kenya (see p. 81), Pius Mutisya and Joseph Kilonzo have successfully produced flat tiles and corrugated sheets of this material by adapting technologies off-project. They have set up in business to sell these products. They found that the addition of red oxide colouring made these tiles more acceptable locally

- In Nepal (see p. 96), Mr Dangi is in full production of micro-concrete tiles using a vibrating table developed by Martin Steinson

- It is only by assessing the rate at which technologies such as those being developed at the Technology Consultancy Centre in Kumasi, Ghana (see p. 102), are taken up by the surrounding community that the success of such projects can be measured

- In St Vincent (see p. 108), Martyn Bennett found that quality control of stabilized earth-block production was difficult to maintain once the team from the UK's Building Research Establishment — who had successfully completed the main training centre buildings — had left the island. Even if this problem could have been solved, this new technology was unlikely to be used in low-cost housing in St Vincent. Careful study of local conditions revealed that the main local problem for people wishing to house themselves was security of tenure of their plot. Timber construction was far more common than blockwork, as timber could be re-used elsewhere if people were forced off their original plot. Hired cranes have been seen moving timber clapboard houses after the service of eviction notices. The establishment of a user committee might have avoided this misapplication of a technology whose success elsewhere had inflated expectations, and

- The manufacture of tools by English, Victorian joiners and wheelwrights for their own use, was the concept behind the work of Aaron Moore when he proposed that Kenyan craftsmen could make their own tools (see p. 88). But these ideas had to be adapted to local conditions and to the tasks and standards of accuracy required by Kenyan builders today. Handmade tools now incorporate principles collected from many sources, adapted to the specific task now on hand in Kenya.

## 5 Linking with government and external funding

There is a debate within the development worker community as to the extent to which a fieldworker should be a conduit for funds from government or an external aid agency to a local community. Many would argue that nothing should be brought in from outside and that the fieldworker should offer only his or her skills, energy and commitment to the host community.

Nevertheless, to this host community, the fieldworker is also a representative of the outside world, and one of that fieldworker's skills is the ability to talk to the world of government and external aid. This is another example of the need for a user-committee to which the development worker can relate. If the local committee do the work, make the decisions about how to get the help they need, and define what form that help should take, then it can be argued that the development worker can justifiably offer advice on how to go about this process.

In those cases where the fieldworker is working directly for government, usually in a planning capacity and without the benefit of a user-committee, then the results have been variable.

○ In Banjul, the capital of Gambia (see p. 99), the low-cost housing project to which Douglas Edwards was attached collapsed when its funding from the United Nations failed to materialize. However, his colleague Richard Blyth, working in the provincial town of Farafenni, found that local planning could be appropriate in controlling and servicing the expansion of towns, and
○ In Belize (see p. 109), Ian Munt found that flexible government planning, particularly to provide landfill for urban expansion, was essential for the incremental growth required by new residents to control their own future.

Most of the postings to date have been to rural areas where it has been easier to identify a user group to which the fieldworker could relate. In the cities, postings have been to government offices and there has been little or no direct contact with the future users of the buildings planned. Designs have been based on statistics gathered on income, average family size and government standards, not on direct contact with the residents. There is now a move towards postings in the informal urban sector. Here, contact with users in the form of a contact committee is an essential ingredient in the development of a truly fruitful relationship, if technologies which are appropriate to the aspirations of the users are likely to be developed.

## 6 Recommendations to aid agencies

**Longer-term commitment** is a better use of an organization's time and is more likely to lead to a successful project than an individual posting. A project cycle geared only to a two-year posting is too short to achieve anything substantial. A team approach with overlapping postings is more likely to be successful.

○ VSO has been involved in Kenya since the early 1960s and with Muka Mukuu since 1983 (see pp. 77–85). The network of skills represented by the agency's large commitment, together with that of similar projects such as those of ITDG and Action-Aid Kenya's Appropriate Technology Unit (now independent of AAK and known as APPROTEC, Kenya), have created a critical mass of expertise available to support the whole range of on-going projects
○ Similarly, since 1986 in Bhutan (see p. 93), a great deal of progress has been made in adjusting projects to both suit the development workers and

75

make the work on the school-building programme more appropriate. This would not have been possible without the cumulative experience of an extended commitment, and

○ The successful posting of Richard Blyth to Farafenni in Gambia (see p. 100), was given a sound foundation by the previous posting of Leif Skule. This was enhanced by arranging a hand-over period.

**More evaluation of projects** would help to identify adequate project support and improve future postings. Greater importance should be given to feasibility and pre-feasibility studies.

This recommendation flows naturally from the one immediately above. Particularly in the field of technical development, it is important for evaluators to look for evidence of spin-off. Spin-off is where innovations introduced on the project are actually adapted and used in the real economy around the project area. This is precisely the kind of multiplier effect which suggests that a particular innovation is viable and useful in the local context. Such developments may give rise to follow-up postings where diversification and lateral development would be the aim, rather than a straightforward replication or replacement approach. At the end of a posting fieldworkers should be asked for their assessment of what project objectives should be pursued by future fieldworkers, and whether these would be followed up by local people.

**Training programmes**, both prior to posting and in-country, should be given higher priority to help familiarize fieldworkers with new materials and alternative techniques.

If the aid agency is to play an enabling role, as described earlier (pp. 65–7), then the methods by which user-group involvement can be used to develop appropriate solutions and adjust and test these in practice will involve the development worker in both teaching and learning. There is therefore a need to expand the development worker's communication skills.

**Asking the fieldworkers** themselves where the work is and what needs doing, should be given greater emphasis.

After an introduction period of around six months, the fieldworker is potentially in the best position to answer these questions. Fieldworkers should be asked to comment, in their reports, on the nature and quality of the work they are doing and to suggest how their posting might be improved.

○ It was by the steady progress made by the development workers in Bhutan (see p. 93) in discovering ways in which their work could be more appropriately based that changes have been made.

These guidelines are not a checklist. The most important guideline to remember is not to impose preconceived solutions. As far as possible, solutions should arise out of the specifics of the situation in which they are to be applied. In the next chapter, we will look at such specifics by examining experience in the field.

## CHAPTER FOUR
# *Experiences In The Field*

## LOW-INCOME BUILDING IN KENYA

*Muka Mukuu Farmers' Co-operative Society's low-cost building project*

Muka Mukuu is a huge coffee and sisal estate, near Thika. It spreads all round the lower slopes of Ol Donyo Sabuk mountain just a few miles from Fourteen Falls on the Athi river. In the days of the White Highlands, the whole estate was held by Lord Northrup McMillan. McMillan's widow sold the estate in the late 1950s. In 1962, just before Kenya's independence, the estate became the property of the co-operative society, representing hundreds of small farmers. It functions now as a representative body, but, in reality, Muka Mukuu is a patchwork of small, individually held farms. Over the years, the small farmers, many of whom were originally classed legally as squatters, have chiefly been interested in obtaining security of tenure of their own *shamba* from the estate. In most cases, this was finally achieved in the early 1980s after a Ministry of Agriculture/GTZ (German Technical Co-operation Agency) joint project to register land rights, revitalize the sisal factory and coffee-processing plant on the estate and improve infrastructure, for example roads, schools, water supply, and dips.

It is an undertaking, therefore, which combines features of individual land-holding with a large, complex co-operative superstructure. The size of the estate can be gauged by the fact that in 1991, it contained 10 primary schools (see Figure 29).

VSO has had a long involvement with Muka Mukuu, dating back to 1983. The involvement with the current low-cost building project, however, dated from 1987, with the arrival of Anne Martin and Andy Bennett. (See also *Using Technical Skills in Community Development*, Dawson 1990, which features a short case-study on the Muka Mukuu low-cost building project.)

1987 was designated by the United Nations as International Year of Shelter for the Homeless (IYSH). In direct response to the IYSH message, the Muka Mukuu Society appealed for assistance to build 10 demonstration houses, one at each of the primary-school sites on the estate. The idea of this was twofold. First, to train local people, especially school-leavers, in income-generating construction skills. And second to help attract teachers to the schools by providing good accommodation for them.

A spin-off might be the uptake of improved, low-cost construction methods, which householders on the estate, most of whom were accustomed

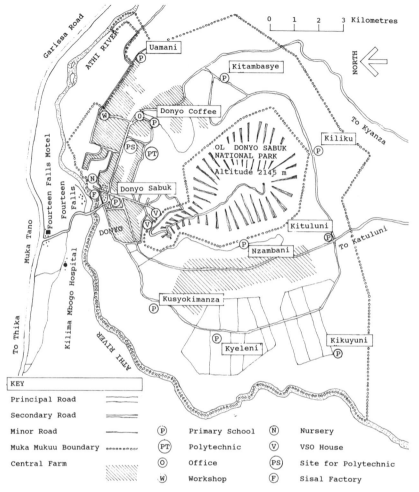

**Figure 29.** *Map of Muka Mukuu, Kenya.*

to regularly building and rebuilding their own *nyumba*, could use in their own house-construction work in the future. A sum of £19,500 was guaranteed by IYSH/UK for the basic implementation of the building programme, with a further sum set aside for the cost and maintenance of a four-wheel-drive vehicle for the project.

Between 1987 and 1991, there were four development workers who worked on this project in a variety of roles: Anne Martin (1987 to 1988), a social survey and communications specialist; Andy Bennett (1987 to 1991), team co-ordinator; Chris Grainger (1988 to 1990), project builder; and Bob Jeffreys, who had already worked for two years as a woodwork teacher at Marsabit in Kenya, and who took over the project co-ordinating role in May

Figure 30. *Andy Bennett and James Kitonyi building teachers'*
*accommodation at Muka Mukuu Farmers' Co-operative in Thika,*
*Kenya. The exterior walls are local stone and the internal partition*
*walls are stabilized earth blocks.*

1991. So what work did this changing team tackle over a five-year period,
and what are the results so far?

It is clear (see Jonathan Dawson, *Using Technical Skills in Community*
*Development*) that the foundations for the work on the low-cost building
project at Muka Mukuu were laid by the painstaking approach adopted by
the first two volunteers. Martin was concentrating on the social survey, and
paying particular attention to the views of women living and working on the
estate. Meanwhile Bennett made a valuable study of local building methods,
materials, costs and possible ways of upgrading the durability of buildings
constructed from locally-available materials.

This participative approach, motivated by a desire to observe and learn,
takes time. Martin, in particular, patiently invested a lot of time and effort
in establishing building committees at each of the 10 primary-school sites,
and in explaining the basis on which it was proposed that the work should
proceed. Although this preparatory work may conflict with a desire for
instant results, it is an essential part of any community builder's work. At
Muka Mukuu, a simple formula was agreed upon and very clearly explained
to all the local volunteers who stepped forward to help build the new
teachers' houses. Local volunteers would give about six weeks' full-time

79

# MUKA MUKUU
# Training Programme

INTERNATIONAL YEAR OF SHELTER FOR THE HOMELESS

# Certificate of Participation

Homeless International is supporting 52 projects worldwide.
Muka Mukuu Training Programme is one of these projects.

In the true spirit of Harambee_____ has participated
in this programme, learning new skills at_____.

Homeless International, Voluntary Services Overseas and the members
of Muka Mukuu Farmers Co-Operative Society, extend their thanks and
congratulations to the participant. We hope that these new skills
will benefit the trainee and the community at large.

The Chairman; Muka Mukuu
Farmers Co-Operative Society. _____.
The Chief; Kyanzavi Location. _____.
The Director; VSO Kenya        . _____.
VSO Builder; Muka Mukuu        . _____.
VSO Co-Ordinator; Muka Mukuu. _____.


Date._____.

Figure 31.   *Muka Mukuu building training certificate.*

80

effort on their local site. In return, they would receive a midday meal, paid for by IYSH funds, six weeks' training in the making and use of stabilized earth blocks, in block-laying, basic masonry, carpentry, tile-making and roofing. They would also receive a certificate of training on completion of the building work (see Figure 31).

However, although the development workers adopted a participatory approach, the project itself had from the outset defined the purpose of the buildings to be constructed. Martin comments that she wishes that the project had left more flexibility in defining the purpose of the buildings, instead of decreeing, in advance, that they would be for teachers' accommodation. She says that the community clearly had other priorities and, indeed, some of the later buildings reflected these or involved a dual use to meet community-determined priorities more fully.

In spite of this, the participatory approach had helped to motivate the community and the work proceeded well. Over a three-year period, more than 50 local people participated in the building work and received basic training in the building skills listed above. By October 1988, one small group who had been trained on the project, had set off on their own to establish a private sisal-cement tile-making unit.

In April 1991, one of the authors of the present study made a second visit to Muka Mukuu specifically to try to learn what spin-off, if any, had taken place. It was found that several of the community volunteers had set up independent production units in the local housing market, using their new skills and often adapting those skills or introducing innovations more suited to local housing needs.

*1 Pius Mutisya and Joseph Kilonzo*
We visited Pius Mutisya and Joseph Kilonzo at the production unit which they were running in space which was rented in an old sisal factory owned by two local businessmen. At the time, the rent and certain other overheads were still being covered by the project, but they were due to go independent, only relying on Bob Jeffreys for occasional technical support, from June to July 1991. They were making sisal-cement tiles, interlocking concrete blocks (which link to make circular rainwater-catchment tanks), and segmented ferro-cement tank covers.

Mutisya was one of the first local volunteers to step forward to build the house at Kusyokimanza school in early 1988. After that, he made stabilized earth blocks and used them to build a hen-house on his own *shamba*, as well as conducting building jobs for friends and neighbours. His *shamba* work continued to take up much of his time at various times of year, but he was always keen to continue his involvement with the project, giving a lot of his time freely. By 1991 he was clearly very keen to develop the production unit into a viable business.

81

Interestingly, Mutisya and Kilonzo have introduced a number of innovations at the production unit, particularly in tile-making.

**Flat-tiles** — they have found that flat tiles were a more attractive proposition than the standard pantile, which is made using a curved plastic mould (designed and patented by J. Parry Limited in England and made under licence in Nairobi). Obviously, the moulds cost money to buy and production of each batch of tiles was restricted by the number of moulds bought. On the other hand, the number of flat tiles (which Mutisya and Kilonzo call slates) which could be made in each batch was only limited by the flat, covered floor area (for stacking) available for the tiles to set on. When fixing the flat tiles, they found that a steeper pitch of roof and a larger degree of overlap between tiles was necessary than was the case with the pantiles, so stronger roof timberwork (more rafters and purlins) was required. They still found the slates more economic and virtually as strong as the pantiles. They cited the fact, also, that the slates were easier to stack, load and transport, with a lower percentage of breakages in transit.

**Mabati tile moulds** — Mutisya has achieved good results in sisal-cement tile-making using corrugated sheeting (*mabati*) in place of the standard curved mould, again at much lower cost, producing a corrugated-tile effect.

**Tile colour** — they found it necessary to add small amounts of red oxide dye to the sand/cement/sisal-fibre mix to produce a tile which was pale pink rather than cement-grey. This was found to be more acceptable to customers.

*2 Peter Ndivo — blockmaking*

Peter Ndivo is another of the community volunteers who started work on the first project house, built at Kusyokimanza in 1988. In 1990, fully two years after he had left the project, he bought his own block-making press for 4000 Kenya shillings.

He used it to build a new house for himself and also to carry out part-time paid work for various neighbours who were keen to emulate his own improved house. When asked how he transported the heavy steel block press to the various sites where he carried out this work, he replied, 'Oh, that's easy, I take the big plank out and then tie the machine on to my bicycle. Then, with some help from the children, I can wheel it anywhere.' Clearly, there's a case here for a wheeled block press.

Ndivo's response to the question 'why do you like this house better than your old one?' was to treat it, frankly, as an incomprehensibly stupid question. He simply regarded it as self-evident that his new house, with its hard, block walls, its windows, its rectangular floor-plan and its thatched verandah was 'better' — and all his neighbours thought so too.

*3 Simon Muinde — compressed earth block construction*

Simon Muinde also worked on the IYSH project. When he built a new house on his *shamba*, he decided that he could build a better, more durable house

Figure 32. *A blockmaking project in Suhum District, Ghana.*

Figure 33. *Simon Muinde and his house.*

if he used some of the new techniques he had learnt while he was working with Andy Bennett and Chris Grainger.

He couldn't afford to buy cement for use as a stabilizer, so he decided to hire Peter Ndivo's block press and build his new house out of compressed earth blocks. By careful selection of soil and particle sizes and, we suspect, adding a small quantity of a local soil that has many of the properties of a natural plaster, he produced a sturdy, well finished and durable dwelling (see Figure 33). The natural plaster is used on the front wall of his house.

Muinde was clear about the advantages of his new house. The walls and floors were smooth and easy to keep clean. He liked the thatched roof which kept his house cool during the heat of the day and wouldn't consider using *mabati*. When he could afford it, he planned to buy some FCR tiles in Ol Donyo and reroof the house — maybe in the mid-1990s.

He showed us the houses of some of his very near neighbours. One group of houses was of the completely traditional Kamba type, with sisal-pole frame, wattle-and-daub walls, thatched grass roof and no windows. This type of house had a doorway, of course, but no door. Muinde reckoned that they would need major repairs after each rainy season and would probably need complete rebuilding after two years, three at most.

Nearer his own house, his next-door neighbour had built a house from sun-dried clay bricks. This house had a rectangular floor-plan, small windows and a fitted, hinged door.

84

Elsewhere on the estate, wealthier members of the community — traders, shop-owners, bar-owners and people who owned a larger *shamba* — had employed builders to construct larger bungalow-type houses with concrete blocks, *mabati* roofs, catchment tanks and internal bathrooms, or at least an outside latrine.

One of the most interesting things about housing at Muka Mukuu was that there was a wide range of existing, possible housing types, all within close proximity. Nobody could possibly afford to move straight from a completely traditional *nyumba* to a bungalow but, with plenty of intermediate types and combinations of improvements in terms of durability and status along the way, people could set themselves realizable targets for housing improvement, if they wanted to.

*Embu Municipal Council — a women's self-help low-cost housing project*
Philip Dorian was posted to Embu in 1989, originally as a roads engineer. However, the council changed its priorities and, in a move which entirely suited Dorian's outlook too, decided that he should pursue an ambitious, urban low-cost building project. The project has attracted a good deal of financial support from Plan International and Action-Aid Kenya.

It was clearly a managed project. The aim was to build a large estate of standard-design dwellings (designed by Dorian and meeting all the building-regulation requirements of the municipality) in two or three phases of 40 to 50 units each. It was envisaged as running over 10 years, from 1990 to 2000 or so.

The workforce consists of local women who become scheme members and are then employed by the project, receiving an unskilled labourer's wage. They receive training in blockmaking and tilemaking. They work at the project's unit, which is located in the compound of the Municipal Council Offices and, in April 1991, had recently begun work on the first experimental house at the main project site in Embu.

It was envisaged that work on the main project site would commence sometime in 1992, working in teams supervised by recognized craftsmen who would be responsible for quality control. Completed houses would become project property and would be allocated to scheme members according to need. The details of the plan had yet to be finalized in mid-1991, but Dorian's view was that women scheme members would need to sign up for a number of years and work through that period before they would have entitlement to taking on a rented house under the scheme.

This project aimed at providing 100 or so new, rented housing units for Embu in the following 10 years, equipping a significant number of women with income-generating skills in the process. Clearly, those were aims which were well worth supporting. Even so, a number of aspects of the scheme appear highly controversial. It looks very top-down. It is not clear how a workforce composed of women, who were all in their 20s and 30s, could realistically be asked to give a commitment to five years' work (unless there were arrangements for sisters to stand in while they were child-bearing, for example). The fact that no scheme member knew whose house they were building at any given time — because the houses were all the same and went into a pool — must have been a problem in terms of motivation. It meant, also, that it was not possible to accommodate changes in design to meet the needs of particular families.

Compounding these problems further, the Embu Municipal Council planned to clear a nearby existing shanty settlement, known as Shauriyako (Swahili for all your fault!), in the immediate future. Clearly, this was one of those projects where it is now (1992) still too early to assess its impact on the workforce in terms of acquisition of skills and on the community in terms of meeting housing need.

*Youth polytechnics: background*
We have attempted to summarize here the experience gained by fieldworkers in the role of trade instructors. Many of these instructors were involved in low-cost building activities, both as trainers and as contractors, and they had to learn a great deal, largely by trial and error, about the market for low-cost buildings in various parts of Kenya.

Youth polytechnics (YPs) are mostly small, village-based trade training schools, usually with about 50 or 60 trainees on their roll. VSO has had a long involvement with the YPs (and the forerunners of the YPs, then known as village polytechnics) dating back to the late 1960s, sending vocational instructors in a variety of trades, including metalwork, carpentry, electrical installation, masonry, building and basic business skills. The vast majority of the 300-plus YPs functioning in 1992 in Kenya rely on *harambee* (that is, popular, local fund-raising initiatives) for their existence.

In the late 1980s and early 1990s, in response to the needs of YP trainees and the economic realities of Kenya itself, the emphasis of VSOs role in the YPs shifted. Attainment of a leaving certificate or even of a Trade Test pass was not enough for YP graduates to have any realistic chance of plying their trade and earning a living at it. Increasingly, it became essential that the YP-leaver was able to function in the informal sector as an independent artisan (or *fundi*). It was therefore vital that they acquired saleable, marketable skills. In most cases, this meant acquiring basic business skills and an ability to work within the challenges and constraints of the informal sector, where the working up of low-cost, locally-available raw materials with a minimum of self-made or low-cost tools would be a prime requirement.

The largest market for the services of the *fundi* was likely to be a market of poor people, whether they were urban- or rural-based, so the skills acquired during their training would need to be geared towards these realities, rather than a training based on the syllabus of the City and Guilds of London Institute and its assumptions which are based on a very different

86

real economy. In this situation, a student's ability to recall from memory and correctly label the parts of a Stanley No. 10 plane was likely to be less important than the ability to acquire a basic set of tools.

Equally, given the constraints of *harambee* fundraising by the local community, it would usually only be possible to get supplies of materials for training purposes on the basis that the trainees, under their instructor, constituted themselves as a workgroup and submitted tenders for actual jobs. In this setting, training and production would go hand in hand.

All of this affected the role of vocational instructors in the YPs, irrespective of their trade, speciality or nationality. As so much of their training work is contract-based, building-trades instructors now needed to learn as much as possible about the economics of local building and the requirements of the market that they are trying to operate in.

**Working in the real economy**

It should be remembered that, in rural areas especially, the economy is not by any means fully a cash economy. A good deal of building, especially of dwellings, may still be done on a basis which involves unpaid co-operation or where payment is by exchange of services, exchange of obligations or payment in kind. Furthermore, significant amounts of materials may have no cash cost (earth, dried grass, sisal poles, and the like). Unless a building instructor understands these things, he will get his economics completely wrong and may be passing unusable skills on to the trainees.

Operating within the cash economy, such as building houses for wealthier rural clients, building extensions to the local shop and so on, the building instructor who is an outsider will need to learn from scratch about the economics of building in another country. Each alternative building material will need to be evaluated afresh, taking into account local economics.

For walling in most areas of Britain, one might well judge kiln-fired bricks to be the best available material, taking durability, finish, workability and cost into account. If one opts for bricks, one picks up the telephone and orders them by the cubic yard. In various parts of Kenya, however, the factors affecting the choice of walling material is likely to be very different. These are some of the questions which might arise:

○ Is local stone available? What does it cost?
○ If stone cannot be quarried on site, is the cost of transporting stone to site too high?
○ Are bricks available or could they be made locally?
○ Does the quality of the building require fired bricks? If so, what is the fuel-wood situation?
○ If bricks are not viable, are local earths suitable for blockmaking? and
○ If so, what stabilizers (for example, cement or lime) will be required, if any?

Each one of these questions can only be answered when local prices and costs are well known. Building instructors working at Youth Polytechnics quickly came to grips with these realities because they were forced to work in the real economy, carrying out contract work.

Interestingly, Nick Hall, who headed the Intermediate Technology Development Group's Nairobi Office and is himself a building craftsman, commented that Kenya was the only country in Africa where rough-dressed building stone — especially where the stone was relatively soft and workable — was a cheaper walling material than stabilized earth. However, given the irregular shapes of rough-dressed stone a greater amount of mortar would be used in walling the same area and, especially where cement is expensive, this would need to be taken carefully into account.

## Producing local machines

Development worker building instructors in Kenya accumulated useful experience using appropriate machinery in the production of building materials. For the stabilized earth as a building material, a number of variations on the original CINVA ram (see p. 38) were used. The Action-Aid Kenya Action Pack Block Press, manufactured in Nairobi by Makiga Engineering Limited (see Figure 34), was the most widely used single model.

A number of development workers were also involved in the production of fibre-cement roofing tiles (FCR tiles) originally using technologies developed by ITDG, and John Parry Limited of Cradeley Heath, West Midlands. More recently, Action-Aid Kenya's tile-making kit, which is again entirely manufactured in Kenya, has been preferred (see Figure 36).

Detailed comment on the use of stabilized earth and FCR tiles is to be found in connection with the housing project at Muka Mukuu on p. 82.

## Availability of tools

Some comment should also be made on the availability of builders' tools. The production of carpenters' handtools is a case in point.

In 1983, Aaron Moore was a carpentry instructor at Kaaga School for the Deaf in Kenya. He realized that one of the constraints on his trainees' ability to set themselves up as craftsmen was the problem of access to tools. Imported machine-made tools from Europe were prohibitively expensive. The solution was, he reasoned, to go back to the time in Britain before the introduction of machine-made hand-tools appeared on the market, and revive the skills of making carpenters' tools by hand, as every apprentice cabinet-maker, joiner, wheelwright and shipwright used to do in Victorian Britain. On his return to Britain from Kenya, Moore put these ideas into action and developed a set of drawings and cutting lists, since published by ITDG, for the manufacture of a full set of tools, including the jack plane, rebate

88

# MAKIGA ENGINEERING WORKS
## P.O. BOX 77593 NAIROBI TEL: 797024

### ACTION PACK BLOCK PRESS

This heavy duty, manually operated, locally manufactured, high compaction block press was designed by Action Aid - Kenya's Appropriate Technology Unit to make

STABILISED SOIL BUILDING BLOCKS

These strong, permanent, low cost, building blocks are made from a mixture of soil and a small portion of cement. After being formed in the press they are cured for a minimum of 7 days before use. Almost any soil that contains both clay and sand can be used and the cost of the blocks is as much as 50% cheaper than other "conventional" walling materials!

Stabilised Soil Blocks are recommended and promoted by:

STABILISED BLOCKS & F.C.R. TILES

- Housing Research Development Unit (HRDU) at University of Nairobi
- Intermediate Technology Development Group (ITDG)
- United Nations Center for Human Settlements (HABITAT)
- Building Research Establihsment (BRE)

There are many buildings in Nairobi and throughout Kenya built with these blocks. The Action Pack Block Press is designed to produce stronger blocks, have a longer life and produce more blocks per day than other block presses available in Kenya. Over 100 Action Pack Presses were sold during the first 18 months of production in Kenya.

Its unique features include:
- Extra High Compaction Pressure
- Adjustable Ratio for different soils
- Double Action Ejection Stroke for easier ejection

ACTION PACK BLOCK PRESS

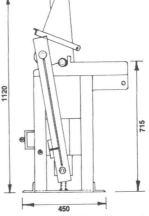

The Action Pack Block Press is an ideal tool for small businesses, building contractors, individuals or self-help groups.

- Block Size
  : 5½" x 4½" x 11½"
  (140 x 115 x 290mm)

- Block Production:
  : Up to 700 blocks per day with 5 workers.

  : 90 to 140 blocks per bag of cement, depending on the soil used.

**FOR MORE INFORMATION CONTACT: MAKIGA ENGINEERING WORKS**
P.O. BOX 77593 NAIROBI TEL: 797024

Figure 34. *Action Pack block press made by Makiga Engineering Works.*

## ACTION PACK BLOCK PRESS

This heavy duty, manually operated, locally manufactured, high compaction block press was designed by ActionAid-Kenya's Appropriate Technology Unit to make
STABILISED SOIL BUILDING BLOCKS
These strong, permanent, low cost, building blocks are made from a mixture of soil and a small portion of cement. After being formed in the press they are cured for a minimum of 7 days before use. Almost any soil that contains both clay and sand can be used and the cost of the blocks is as much as 50% cheaper than other "conventional" walling materials!

Stabilised Soil Blocks are recommended and promoted by:
- Housing Research Development Unit (HRDU) at University of Nairobi
- Intermediate Technology Development Group (ITDG)
- United Nations Center for Human Settlements (HABITAT)
- Building Research Establishment (BRE)

There are many buildings in Nairobi and throughout Kenya built with these blocks.

The Action Pack Block Press is designed to produce stronger blocks, have a longer life and produce more blocks per day than other block presses available in Kenya. Over 100 Action Pack Presses were sold during the first 18 months of production in Kenya.

Its Unique Features include
- Extra High Compaction Pressure
- Adjustable Compaction Ratio for different soils
- Double Action Ejection Stroke for easier ejection

The Action Pack Block Press is an ideal tool for small businesses, building contractors, individuals or self-help groups.

- Manufactured by : Undugu Society of Kenya
  Metal Production Unit
  P.O. Box 40417, Nairobi

  Tel: 552211, 540187

- Price : 10,000 Ksh.

- Block Size : 5½" x 4½" x 11½" (140 x 115 x 290 mm)

- Block Production : Up to 700 blocks per day with 5 workers

  : 90 to 140 blocks per bag of cement, depending on the soil used.

Potential Profits from Selling Blocks: Up to 1,000 Ksh per day if soil is free.

For more information and training on how to manufacture and build with Stabilised Soil Blocks contact:
ActionAid-Kenya
Appropriate Technology Unit
P.O. Box 42814 — NAIROBI
Phone: 743000/799989/799993

### INFORMATION SHEET

Figure 35.  *Action-Aid information sheet on Action Pack block press.*

## *ActionAid-Kenya* ⬤ *Appropriate Technology Unit*

## FIBRE-CONCRETE ROOFING TILE MACHINES

These robust, locally manufactured machines were designed by ActionAid-Kenya's Appropriate Technology Unit to make

### FIBRE-CONCRETE ROOFING (FCR) TILES

These low-cost, attractive and durable tiles make a cool, quiet roof which costs as little as 30 gauge corrugated iron (mabati) roof, even when extra timber, labour and transport costs are included. FCR Tile production is an ideal activity for small businesses, buildings contractors or self-help groups.

- Tile Size: 250mm x 500mm
- Thickness: 6mm or 8mm
- Coverage: 12½ tiles per m²
- Production: - up to 300 tiles per day, with 5 workers
  - 120 tiles per bag of cement
- Start-up Costs: Under 30,000 Ksh, including machinery, accessories, 250 moulds, water tanks and 6 weeks working capital.
- Potential Profits: Up to 450Ksh per day.

Pioneered by Intermediate Technology Workshops in the early 1980's, FCR Tile technology achieves lightweight yet strong tiles by using a vibrating table to compact a 3:1, sand: cement mortar (mixed with a small portion of sisal fibre) into a flat screed. The thin, compacted screed is placed onto a mould for 12 hours to give it its shape, and is then cured for 10 days in water tank. FCR Tile making can easily be mastered in a week long training course, offered by ActionAid-Kenya.

ActionAid-Kenya has promoted FCR tile production since 1983. They have:

- Assisted Primary Schools to roof over 200 buildings with FCR Tiles.
- Designed FCR Tile machines and moulds for local manufacture which sell for **less than 15% the price of imported equipment.** (Over 150 machines were sold in Kenya the first 18 months of production).

FCR Tiles are also promoted in Kenya by:

- Kenya Bureau of Standards
- Housing Research Development Unit (HDRU), University of Nairobi
- Intermediate Technology Development Unit (ITDG)
- United Nations Center for Human Settlements (HABITAT)

To date, several housing estates have been built in Kenya using FCR Tiles.

**ELECTRIC TILE MACHINE:** This compact electrical vibrating table is powered by a single 12-volt car battery. It requires minimal maintenance, ut the battery needs recharging once a week. Price: 4,500 Ksh. (without battery).

**PEDAL POWERED TILE MACHINE:** This heavy duty pedal powered vibrating machine is for use in rural areas, where labour is cheaper and access to battery charging is limited. It is easily maintained by any bicycle mechanic. Price: 8,800 Ksh.

**Manufactured by:**

Makiga Engineering Works
P.O. Box 77593, NAIROBI
Tel: 797024 (Hse) 766714

Undugu Society of Kenya
Metal Production Unit
P.O. Box 40417, NAIROBI
Tel: 552211 / 540187

**Tile Moulds locally manufactured by:**

James Mtuy
Tiles and Moulds Maker
P.O. Box 11785, NAIROBI
TEL: 766714

For more information and training on FCR Tile manufacture and use, contact:

ActionAid - Kenya
Appropriate Technology Unit
P.O. Box 42814 - NAIROBI
Phone: 799989 / 799993 / 743000

━━━━━ INFORMATION SHEET ━━━━━

Figure 36. *Action-Aid information sheet on FCR tiles.*

91

planes, block plane, mortise gauge, chisels, cramps and work benches (Moore 1986, 1987).

Moore had also designed a two-week training course on tool-making techniques, which now includes techniques of forgework to produce plane irons and chisel blades in a small charcoal forge, using scrap spring steel as the raw material. Since 1988, volunteer carpenters have regularly attended this course before departure overseas, so that they can offer training in these techniques. A similar course, jointly sponsored by ITDG and VSO in blacksmiths' tool-making was also introduced.

By April 1991, volunteer builders in Kenya were beginning to ask what could be done to introduce the small-scale production of quarrying, masonry and blocklaying tool-making technologies, such as cold chisels, bolsters, floats, trowels, and so on.

Steven Payne, who in 1991 was the co-ordinator of the YTSP (see below) was formerly a metalwork and blacksmith instructor at Rapogi YP in South Nyanza. While there, he worked up drawings and produced, with his trainees, a number of serviceable blockmaking presses using welded mild steel from stock.

*The Youth Training Support Programme (YTSP)*

The YTSP is a special initiative, funded by the EEC and administered under the Kenyan Ministry of Technical Training and Applied Technology, in which VSO Kenya is involved. It has aimed to provide in-service training to YP instructors, business skills training to YP graduates who were aiming to set up their own businesses, and various other short courses.

It was formally established in 1990 and, while some courses were already running by mid–1991, the major aspect of work was the actual construction of four YTSP training centres: at Keroka (near Kisii), Wote (near Makueni), Kiirua (Meru District) and Bushiangala (near Kisumu). At each of these sites, a development worker acted as a building co-ordinator and was chiefly responsible for all aspects of the building work. Although funding was not as restricted as it was for the YP instructors, it was noticeable that it was still the social aspect of the work which proved to be the most demanding.

For example, the biggest problem for Richard Skitch at Wote was the initial difficulty of securing a water supply for building work on a hilltop site some kilometres from the trading centre of Makueni. Before he could build ferro-cement rainwater catchment tanks, he had to become involved in contracts with the local owners of ox-carts and donkey-carts to transport 45-gallon drums of water up to the site. He freely admitted that, when he arrived in Kenya, he just wasn't expecting to have to solve problems which he considered to be so basic and, by implication, which he felt lay outside his remit. It should perhaps be added that many builders recruited by development agencies have had to solve much more basic problems than that.

At Keroka, Brian Marler, who had already worked as a building instructor at Moyo Technical Institute in northern Uganda, found that the site earmarked for the YTSP training centre was similarly inaccessible in terms of transport. His real problem, though, was over the allocation of land, as he discovered as soon as perimeter fencing was erected.

Despite promises that the YTSP site had been allocated with the full backing of the ministry and the local MP, local farmers protested that the hilltop land might not be very productive, but that it was rightly theirs. How could an outsider possibly proceed to build a communal facility in a farming community some distance from the main road linking the towns of Kisii and Kericho without solid community support?

Marler's approach was to set up a number of village meetings and discussions with individual farmers, in which he set about explaining that he could not proceed if there was no local support for the project. He pointed out the possible advantages in terms of training for employment for the sons and daughters of the local families. Some families, whose land actually abutted the YTSP site, or who claimed that they had been deprived of land, were promised that fees for their son or daughter to attend courses at the centre could be waived. An amicable agreement was reached. Marler said that, in his view, building work could not have commenced otherwise and that the period of village meetings was the most difficult part of the project, but it was also the most rewarding. After that, he said, people knew what the centre was all about and there was eventually a sense, admittedly very late and in an unplanned way, of community involvement.

From that point onwards, the centre sprang up. Local people were hired and trained to do the building, learning new skills as they went along. Stabilized earth blocks were used above the damp-proof course, and FCR tiles, which were made on site, were to be used for the roofs. All the setting out was done by water-level. VIP (ventilated improved pit) latrines were constructed on site at an early stage.

Potentially, all these new skills were now available within the local community for house-building and other purposes. In 1991 it was too early to tell whether this had taken off. It would take a number of years more before an assessment of that kind could be made.

## LOW-INCOME BUILDING IN THE HIMALAYAS

### Bhutan

In Bhutan, 10 VSOs have worked in various capacities in the national school-building programme since 1986. They have worked within the School Planning and Building Cell (SPBC), a part of the Department of Education, which has its headquarters at Thimphu, Bhutan's capital city. In recent years, Bhutan has placed an emphasis on making education accessible to the

93

mass of the people, and this has involved an ambitious school-building programme and a more systematic approach to the maintenance and repair of existing schools.

Rob Fielding, working alongside civil engineer John Blaney, was the founding architect of the SPBC between 1986 and March 1989. Michael Etherton, who was field director in Bhutan from 1988 until 1991, commented that Fielding clearly had a great interest in traditional Bhutanese architecture and made a careful study of its main features and principles of construction. This turned out to be of considerable help in understanding the country's climate, culture and technology.

This traditional architecture ranks among the most impressive in the world. The big, castle-like *dzong* complexes — fortified, adminsitrative centres, often enclosing a *lhakang* (Buddhist temple) — can only be described as beautifully proportioned and expertly built. They are reminiscent of the Tibetan architecture of the lama caste and, in Bhutan too, it is the monks who are the repository of the drawing-less Bhutanese architectural tradition.

The vernacular architecture of many areas of Bhutan is no less impressive. Traditional stone houses are often built, with great skill, on steeply sloping sites. Joinery skills are of the highest order. In other areas, timber-frame construction, with beautifully carved decoration and rammed-earth in-fill walls, is the order of the day. Sadly, in modern, commercial-sector, public-sector and external donor-funded construction projects, little regard is paid to these fine, indigenous traditions, and there can be a great deal of pressure to use imported, system-built solutions in the interests of getting work completed as quickly as possible.

*Development of VSOs role within the SPBC*
Rob Fielding was followed by a group of four volunteer civil engineers and site supervisors who, between 1987 and 1990, were based at the SPBC headquarters at Thimphu. During this time, both the World Bank and UNESCO/UNICEF came forward with major funding to support particular aspects of the SPBCs work.

As is so often the case in an area where technical experts are involved in work which is, at the end of the day, designed to meet community needs, the clear, majority view of the development workers based at SPBCs Thimphu office was that it was impossible to carry out their role effectively unless they had a greater involvement with local communities. They stressed the need for a clear training role, with specific responsibility for training up identified Bhutanese building engineers and site supervisors, who are currently qualified at diploma level. A meeting of the four workers in the SPBC officially put these views forward, through the field office, to the SPBCs senior personnel in September 1989. At around the same time, one of the workers, Val Ryan, also expressed the view that there should be a greater emphasis, in the agency's role within the SPBC, on Appropriate

94

Technology; that is utilizing, adapting and upgrading local skills, materials and techniques of building, wherever appropriate, instead of routinely falling back on the use of western solutions.

In the period ahead, however, it seems that VSO Bhutan will be keen to work with even more remote school-building projects, which may not always be supported by external donors, and where, for reasons both of funding and of sheer inaccessibility, the need for a heavy emphasis on the use of local skills, low-cost materials and appropriate design will be even greater.

In July 1990, there were just over 70 000 pupils in Bhutan attending 10 high schools, 21 junior schools, 156 primary schools, 46 so-called extended classrooms and eight institutes of higher technical training, including the newly-established National Technical Training Institute (NTTI) and its agricultural equivalent, the NATI. There were development workers at both of the latter.

## Extended classrooms

The extended classrooms, which are also described in recent UNESCO surveys as remote schools, deserve further explanation. These are remote, parent-built classrooms, usually attached, for administrative purposes, to a distant primary school. VSO Bhutan has been very interested in becoming much more involved in providing technical assistance to the building, extension and maintenance of these genuinely community-based institutions. It seemed likely that there would be scope for the development of low-cost building methods in these schools in circumstances which might well lend themselves to certain improvements in building method being adapted informally to family housing in the area — either through self-build or through local artisans taking up some of the methods in the course of their work.

Indeed, by May 1991, we learned that Save the Children Fund (UK) was in the process of assisting in the construction of six extended classrooms or community schools. In May 1991, three of these were nearing completion. Andrew Greenwood, in addition to his main duties at Pema Gatshel, had made two site visits to the fourth of these schools, which was being built at Nyaskar, to offer his technical assistance. Here, the community were building a four-classroom school which would eventually take 130 children.

## Nepal

VSO sent water engineers to work on rural water-supply projects throughout the 1970s and 1980s. Many of these engineers worked closely with local building contractors on projects which involved trenching, wall construction (for spring protection, break tanks, and so on), concrete spillways and other related works.

More recently, however, VSO had involvement in two projects which were specifically aiming at the development and upgrading of uses of traditional building techniques and materials. One of these projects has involved a low-cost housing adviser, Lucky Lowe, who worked at the Appropriate Technology Unit (ATU) at Tulsipur from 1989 until June 1991. The other project of particular interest here was the Earthquake Affected Areas Reconstruction and Rehabilitation Project (EAARRP) where Jim Ford and Holly Robson worked from September 1990 — Ford as a construction-materials specialist and Robson as a communications and publicity adviser.

*The Appropriate Technology Unit, Tulsipur, Dang Province*
In 1991 there were four ATUs in Nepal, working on the development of low-cost roofing tiles, stabilized earth blocks, reinforced-concrete door-frames (and other ways of reducing the amount of expensive timber used in buildings), smokeless chulos (household stoves) and other projects. Lucky Lowe was based at the Dang ATU from early 1989 until mid-1991, and another development worker, Martin Steinson, had been working at the same project from 1986 until 1988.

On her return to Britain in late July 1991, Lowe talked to VSO about the two years she had spent working at Tulsipur and assessed what, in her view, had been achieved during that time. First, she commented on one aspect of Steinson's work. He had clearly done a considerable amount of work on micro-concrete tile making (similar to FCR tiles, see p. 88) and had designed and built a pedal-driven vibrating table — required to achieve a strong, air-bubble-free mix of sand and cement for making these relatively thin tiles.

A small, private enterprise tile-making unit, owned by Mr Dangi, was still in full production, using the techniques and equipment passed on to Mr Dangi while Steinson was in Tulsipur. Lowe reported that the tiles were in demand, especially in the commercial sector, for roofing shops in the bazaar for example.

Lowe's own work on building materials had been aimed at producing stabilized earth blocks that, unlike the locally-favoured burnt bricks, would not entail the use of fuel wood. The block production, although getting off to a promising start, had to be abandoned due to the lack of a market for them locally.

Lowe had been asked to work on production and testing of stabilized earth blocks, using an Indian Bal Ram block press and then to compare these earth blocks for cost and durability with the fired bricks available from many local brickmakers, who fire them in small temporary clamp kilns. Lowe reported that, after thorough experimentation with various soil mixes, blocks were sent to the Engineering Institute at Kathmandu for testing and performed extremely well for strength. They also compared reasonably well for price with locally-produced burnt bricks.

She had actually built a small, demonstration weavers' workshop in Tulsipur, using these blocks (sand:earth:cement in a 15:5:2 mix). There was a great deal of interest in the workshop. People liked its appearance and the

96

Figure 37.  *Micro-concrete roofing tiles and stabilized earth blocks being used to build a demonstration workshop in Tulsipur.*

fact that, whereas bricks vary enormously in their shape, dimensions and hardness, these blocks were neat, sharp-edged and uniform, producing a pleasing visual effect.

However, the stumbling block was identifying a market for these blocks. They were still too expensive for the vast majority of rural people, who continued to build their own houses from locally-available, free materials, namely bamboo, thatch, sun-dried clay bricks, mud construction (pise-style) or the wattle-and-daub style of the indigenous Tharu people. (Further north, in the Gurkha areas, for example, small houses would be made of stone and slate.) The only conceivable market for these blocks in the Dang area, therefore, was in the commercial sector, for building and rebuilding works in the bazaar. The problem here, however, was that nearly all bazaar buildings were two storeys tall, and their walls were therefore almost entirely exposed to the rain. In those circumstances, the water-resistance of burnt clay bricks is much higher than that of stabilized earth, unless expensive and time-consuming rendering is applied. Lowe concluded that there simply was therefore no viable local market for earth blocks.

*The Earthquake Affected Areas Reconstruction and Rehabilitation Project*
The EAARRP was set up by the Nepal Government, under the Ministry of Housing and Physical Planning, shortly after the earthquake of 21 August 1988, with a remit of focusing on reconstruction and repair of damaged schools throughout the earthquake-affected areas of Nepal. Although rated as moderate in scale, the earthquake had caused extensive damage to housing, as well as the social and physical infrastructure of Eastern and Central Nepal. Measured in terms of the number of people affected, the most severe damage was in private housing, followed by school buildings. About 66 000 houses were damaged beyond repair, and more than 1900 schools were destroyed and over 270 badly affected by the earthquake, according to an official government report, *Outline of an Action Plan for the Reconstruction and Rehabilitation of Earthquake Affected Schools* (HMG Nepal; MHPP-EAARRP, Kathmandu, 1988). Reportedly, a few districts lost all their schools.

The EAARRP was thus established with the aim of enabling as many pupils to return to school as quickly as possible. In the process of repair and reconstruction, a number of specific objectives were to be borne in mind.

○ Wherever possible, and bearing in mind that many schools had been built by the voluntary labour of the communities concerned, low-cost building techniques and locally available materials were to be used as widely as possible
○ At the same time, this objective should not be allowed to compromise the need for reinforcement wherever this was necessary to protect against the effects of future earthquakes

o As well as reinforcement, priority should be given to the use of lightweight building elements (roofs, lintels, beams and so on) in view of the fact that fatalities usually occur when occupants of buildings are crushed or trapped beneath heavy building debris

o Except in the northern areas, where the climate is especially cold, the EAARRP building teams (usually an overseer and a mason/builder who would mobilize local people for repair and reconstruction work) would seek to erect at least a well-constructed roofed space, with solid foundations and reinforced corners, large enough for two classrooms, with a temporary partition wall between the two, sill-high curtain walls, and doorways, all round. Permanent brick or masonry walls, windows and external doors could be added by community effort later, and

o In the course of construction, training in earthquake-protection techniques would be given to local voluntary workers from the community. The aim was that they should incorporate some of these measures into the construction of more safely-constructed homes for their own families.

## LOW-INCOME BUILDING IN WEST AFRICA

### Gambia

In February 1988, two development workers were posted to the Ministry of Physical Planning and Housing (MPPH) in the Gambia. Douglas Edwards was posted as a housing officer, based at the headquarters in Banjul, and Richard Blyth was posted as a town planner, based up-country at Farafenni.

The original objectives of the Banjul posting were spelt out clearly in Edward's original project assessment. The tasks were threefold. First, working within the Housing Unit at HQ, Edwards would be required to collect and analyze data on housing conditions, overcrowding, affordability, income-and-expenditure patterns of families in different housing areas of Greater Banjul and other urban centres, liaising with other organizations (such as the Central Statistics Office) as necessary. Secondly, he was to assist the resident GTZ (German Technical Co-operation Agency) adviser on in-service training of housing and building technicians. Finally, and crucially, he was to work on an ambitious low-cost housing project.

This was essentially a basic site-and-services project in the peri-urban area of Greater Banjul and included the building of a small number of demonstration low-cost houses in the rural growth centres of Basse and Farafenni. The emphasis was on enabling people to build better houses using local materials.

In reality, this project was heavily dependent on external funding by the UN housing agency, Habitat, and, when it became clear that the planned US$750,000 funding would not be available, the original objectives of this particular project became no longer viable.

Richard Blyth, on the other hand, was put in charge of one of the branches of the Ministry of Physical Planning and Housing (MPPH) at Farafenni. Blyth undoubtedly benefited from the previous experience gained by another town planner, Leif Skule, who had undertaken a similar posting, based at Basse, for nearly two years before Blyth arrived in Farafenni. Blyth and Skule had the opportunity to meet several times and discuss objectives before Skule left the Gambia.

Farafenni is a town of about 10 000 people, 200 kilometres up the River Gambia from Banjul. The area covered from the Farafenni office was the central part of the Republic of the Gambia, consisting of river, swamp, dry farmland and bush. All 4000 square kilometres of this area lies below 50m altitude and has a total population of about 200 000. Farafenni is the largest town in the district.

The district is predominantly rural, but in 1991 the towns were growing quickly. Farafenni was undergoing especially rapid growth because it stands at the crossroads of the road going along the north bank of the river and the Transgambia Highway, which links north and south Senegal.

The growth of population meant an outward spread in the built-up area around Farafenni. The MPPH's branch office was established in 1985 in response to this situation. Blyth explained that: 'The expansion of trade in the town has meant that space originally set aside for traders in the markets and street frontages has been exhausted and temporary structures have been erected on highway verges.'

The Planning Office at Farafenni commented on lease applications from all over the district from a planner's viewpoint but, in 1991, was concentrating on the Farafenni area itself. Towards the end of Blyth's posting, in November 1989, the office was involved in the revision of the draft Physical Development Plan for Farafenni which was produced in 1985 with the help of GTZ. This plan included cost estimates for the upgrading of existing residential and commercial areas and proposed a considerable expansion of the areas allocated for residential development. The branch office was engaged on detailed layouts for new residential areas.

Blyth's comments on this were very interesting:

Town planning in the developing world is often charged with being too grandiose. Residential layouts produced by the Department of Physical Planning of the Gambia avoid this charge. It is possible for the uptake of land to be halted until a layout is prepared. The layout gives the boundaries of each plot, the use of each plot and the route and width of roads. People may then occupy the plots on payment of the appropriate fee and build structures as they can afford — of reed matting, corrugated metal, mud or cement block.

This layout system has the advantage of causing residential development to occur only in suitable locations with an adequate road network along which water pipes may be laid when money permits. But it does not impose such planning standards as would cause most development to bypass the planning process altogether.

More recently, in September 1990, Simon Addyman arrived at Brikama to work as a construction co-ordinator on a community-based school-building project which was funded by the World Bank. The project objectives assumed a large degree of community involvement in the construction of the school, with voluntary labour in return for training in construction skills. Since Addyman's arrival, VSO has been requested to recruit two other construction co-ordinators, to work on similar ventures at Mansakonko and Kerewan.

## Ghana

Development workers in Ghana in recent years have been working in three different kind of projects which have a direct bearing on the subjects of this study.

o Keith Morley worked as a technical instructor at Kumenda Teacher Training College, having previously worked as a VSO carpentry instructor at a Youth Polytechnic in Kenya
o Deborah Perry worked at the Technology Consultancy Centre, Kumasi, as a buildings-materials specialist, concentrating on fired brick and FCR tile-production techniques, and
o Gerry Gallagher worked as a trade instructor at Volta School for the Deaf.

### Keith Morley: Kumenda TTC

Morley was posted to Kumenda in April 1989. His duties were mainly to teach a range of technical subjects (including building and carpentry) to second- and third-year technical students, most of whom would go on to become junior secondary school teachers, with a significant amount of technical teaching included in their weekly timetables. His approach was to try to communicate the message that teaching must be related to the needs of real life and the real conditions that teachers will face. Morley's earlier experience in Kenya meant that he had an appreciation of the need to look for low-cost, locally-available materials, wherever possible, given restricted budgets and the even tighter budgetary controls that would be likely to face trainee teachers when they entered the local schools.

In keeping with this approach, given the availability of good brick-making clay in many areas of Ghana, he introduced the teaching of brick-making, making wooden brick-moulds. The idea was that student teachers would take the moulds with them when they went on teaching practice and when they became qualified teachers, so that pupils could become involved in community-based initiatives to build new classrooms, workshops and other buildings. The fact that Morley built a house for himself and his family using

101

local materials greatly appealed to the students, and raised the credibility and status of low-cost building techniques.

*Deborah Perry: Kumasi TCC*

Deborah Perry was recruited in 1988 to work as a projects officer in the Ceramics Section of the Technology Consultancy Centre (TCC), which is an institution — with a worldwide reputation in the field of appropriate and intermediate technologies — attached to the University of Kumasi. TCC was specifically established by the Ghanaian government to promote technologies which had been developed at the Ministry of Science and Technology among Ghanaian small industrialists, by setting up pilot schemes and providing training and outreach services. While Perry was at the TCC, the ceramics section were working in three main areas; the development of refractory materials for furnace linings (for small-scale foundries), small-scale burnt-brick manufacture, and the production of FCR tiles (known here as micro-concrete roofing tiles).

As well as solving technical problems relating to the production of the tiles, Perry was heavily involved in the extension work aspects, working with local small-scale entrepreneurs and the Department of Rural Housing on the actual establishment of new tile-making units, with follow-up visits to assist with teething probems and quality control. The work of the ceramics section to promote micro-concrete tiles received recognition and a big boost when the Department of Rural Housing and Cottage Industries decided, with UNDP and ILO financial support, to establish a focal point initiative at the TCC for the promotion of these technologies on a wider basis.

In collaboration with a private brick-producer, the ceramics section successfully established a commercial pilot brick project a few kilometres outside the Kumasi campus. The production of a clay-mixer and a sawdust-bricqueting machine, which were essential to the success of the small-scale brick-making package, was also under way at one of the TCCs sister institutions, the Suame Intermediate Technology Unit.

*Gerry Gallagher: Volta School for the Deaf, Hohoe*

Gallagher said that most of his trainees would seek work as carpenters or as masons when they left school. The carpenters would either specialize as cabinet-makers or as construction carpenters and roofers.

The furniture-makers would produce small household items, aiming ultimately to set up a small workshop, displaying items for sale in the open air outside it. Availability of tools was going to be a major constraint for them. The construction carpenters would hope to get work erecting small shops and stalls, made from timber with iron-sheet roofs.

In the Hohoe area, according to Gallagher, whereas the carpenters would almost certainly have had to set themselves up with a living, the masons would have had a much better chance of gaining formal employment, working for various contractors. He mentioned three government construction organizations: the State Construction Corporation (SCC), the State Housing Corporation (SHC) and the Rural Housing and Cottage Industries. Gallagher added: 'This last offers to build houses for anyone who can supply the materials and then collects payment for labour later.' There would also be chances of employment with the various municipal Public Works Departments.

There would also be a demand for masons' skills in house-building on a one-off basis for individuals. Said Gallager:

> Some houses are built with mud blocks. They are more common in the rural areas, but there are still a few in a largish town like Hohoe. Masons are asked to construct these as well as making the blocks. The blocks are made in a wooden mould using clay and water with a little lime. The lime gives the clay a little more cohesion, preventing it cracking. These mud houses have thatch or corrugated sheet roofs, and have packed earth or screeded floors. Fired bricks and consolidated blocks are known (in this area) but not common.

## LOW-INCOME BUILDING IN SOUTHERN AFRICA

### Zambia

In Zambia, we focus on the work of two development workers: Nicholas Osborne, who has been working as a building engineer with the Smallholder Development Project at Luanshya, and Peter Labouchere, who has been managing a co-operatively owned brick-making plant at Chililabombwe.

*Nicholas Osborne: Smallholder Development Project, Luanshya*
Osborne was posted to Luanshya in October 1989, along with two other colleagues, shortly after completing the VSO/ITDG Appropriate Technology Course. The Smallholder Development Project was funded by the EECs European Development Fund, via the Zambian Ministry of Agriculture and Water Development. In the Luanshya area it aimed to take an integrated approach, raising crop outputs and improving infrastructure, including roads, water supply, health-care and housing conditions.

Luanshya is in Zambia's Copperbelt. As employment in the mines continued to decline, many heads of families were returning the short distance to their home villages. Naturally, this produced pressure for change and for improvements in the quality of life available on the land.

After his arrival at Luanshya, Osborne was involved in site supervision and engineering duties connected with the construction of three types of house, described respectively as high cost, medium cost and low cost, and in liaison with local Zambian contractors on new build and renovation work.

103

Figure 38. *The Kasapa Brickmaking Co-operative in Zambia.*

He decided to start production of blocks on site instead of buying these in. Osborne has also had some involvement with related schemes such as self-help school building.

In his annual report (September 1990), he summarized the work done in his first year at Luanshya and drew attention to some of the main problems — almost all of them being social rather than technical in nature. In the previous year, the project plan had called for the building of two high-cost houses (designated as Type 425), four medium-cost houses (Type 315) and 10 low-cost houses (Type 204). Despite delays in the arrival of imported materials and other transport-related delays, one high-cost house was completed and the other was nearing completion. At the end of the year, three of the four medium-cost houses were described as nearing completion, whilst the fourth was up to wall-plate (roof) level. However, the picture was not so good for the low-cost houses.

Of the 10 planned, only two, at Chowa and Ibenga, were near completion. Lack of serviceable transport for materials had been a recurring problem and, in the end, it had been decided that the building contract would be revamped to a labour-only contract, with transport then being provided by the project (that is, the client) itself.

A third house, at Munkumpu, had had its footings dug. Work on the other seven had not even started, and a decision was finally taken to hand the construction of these over to a new contractor.

Osborne described progress on the self-help school building during his first year at Luanshya as 'very disappointing'. He said that this was mainly due to the villagers' lack of interest when the time came to implement the work. At Chowa, work progressed as far as the completion of the concrete footings. At Shinwa, the classroom block had been set out but still awaited the local community to carry out the excavation work. At Mfulabonga Primary School, the footings had been dug but the project was waiting for the recipients to obtain aggregate for the concrete works. At Butikili, the excavation work for the footings was still in progress, along with the collection of aggregate from local sources.

Osborne went on to explain:

> Early on in the building programme, blocks were purchased from outside the project area and transported to the site. Due to a 20 per cent breakage of blocks, it was decided to purchase block-making moulds and a regular supply of crushed stones so as to start producing both 150mm and 200mm blocks on site. This not only saved time but also reduced the price of a block.

> Two separate blockmaking gangs were established — one on site and the other at the project office. Between them, they were then able to make up to 400 blocks a day, which was adequate for all the building requirements throughout the project area.

*Peter Labouchere: Kasapa Brick-making Co-operative, Chililabombwe*
Labouchere arrived at Chililabombwe in September 1989 to take on the role of production manager/business adviser to the long-established Kasapa Brick-making Co-operative, located in the Kasapa brickfield, where good brickmaking clay exists in abundance. The co-operative was in dire straits when Labouchere arrived, and had been close to bankruptcy for more than 18 months. It had been forced to sell off more and more of its assets, including machinery and transport, to stave off creditors and pay wages to the co-operative members. Liquidation was only avoided in the final quarter of calendar year 1989 by the quick sale of October's brick production (14 000 bricks), coupled with a grant of 28 000 kwacha from VSO Zambia. The co-operative had always had a basically good product, but its problems lay in the areas of marketing and reliability of machinery and, therefore, of delivery dates.

At Labouchere's suggestion, the co-operative applied to the US-based ADF (African Development Fund) for a business development grant. In the meantime, it took out a large, long-term commercial loan via a Zambian organization, Small-scale Enterprise Promotions Limited.

During the dry season, Labouchere addressed the problems of production management of the brick-making process. In the rainy season, he got down to long-term planning, staff training in administration and production, overhauling machinery and plant and, above all, marketing.

The ADF orginally queried whether the co-operative had taken sufficient steps to combat deforestation and they asked for evidence that a planned felling and replanting programme was being followed. With these assurances, the ADF came forward in 1990 with a grant of $70,000. Needless to say, this has meant that the co-operative did not have to live from hand to mouth, but was able to develop its work practices and expand its production considerably.

In the main, its customers were from within the commercial sector. The aim was that the co-operative should become a major local employer and the provider of high-quality burnt-clay bricks for the construction industry in western Zambia.

## Zimbabwe

In 1991 a number of very interesting developments in the upgrading of low-cost building materials and low-cost housing design were taking place in Zimbabwe. ITDG Zimbabwe was promoting work on coal-fired small-scale brick production. This was in response to the availability of coal reserves in Zimbabwe and the need for careful conservation to minimize the use of fuelwood. It was also involved in plans for some ambitious joint initiatives with large employers on the planning and construction of low-cost housing developments for factory workers.

Zimbabwe's Blair Institute has been known since the 1930s for its work on low-cost sanitation options and related rural health-promotion programmes. In addition, at Melfort, just outside Harare, there was a very interesting permanent exhibition site showing traditional Shona and Ndebele houses and displaying ways in which, still using traditional skills and locally-available materials, they could be upgraded. All of these sources provided a potentially stimulating background against which aid-agency builders and planners could play a constructive part.

In 1991 VSO started to post architects and planners to Zimbabwe, but here we will focus on the work of the mason/bricklayers.

### Paul Hill: Mwenezi DTC

Paul Hill worked at two different projects in Zimbabwe. From January 1989 until early 1991 he worked as a building instructor/supervisor at the Mwenezi Development Training Centre at Neshuro in southern Zimbabwe. After that he moved, again as a building instructor, to work at St Joseph's Youth Training Centre at Makore, in Bikita District off the main Masvingo to Birchenough Bridge road.

Hill's actual employer at Mwenezi DTC, Neshuro was a Zimbabwean charity called Glen Forest. His role was to press ahead with the construction of a large rural training-centre complex — to include dormitories, teachers' accommodation, classrooms, workshops and halls — working from a complicated

106

Figure 39. *A large round house being built at Neshuro, Mwenezi District, Zimbabwe.*

design brief and detailed drawings provided by a commercial firm of architects based in Harare.

In the course of constructing these buildings the idea was that Hill would also provide on-the-job training to youths recruited from the surrounding villages, equipping them with some income-generating skills or, at least, the ability to construct better, more durable dwellings for their families, on a self-build basis. These youths would normally attend a course for about six weeks, before returning to their farms and villages, though many would then be able to return for further training within a few months or so.

The majority of the building materials for the construction of the new training centre had to be made on site. Neither the price nor the availability of cement was a problem for this particular project and the type of blocks chosen was sandcrete blocks.

One interesting feature of the work Hill did while he was at Neshuro was the building, with his trainees, of a large teachers' house to a circular floor-plan. It is a large, sandcrete block building with a thatched roof. It was built partly because Hill found the designs of the architect to be very complicated and demanding for his trainees to set out and build, and partly because he wanted to see whether such a building might raise the status of the traditional African *rondevel* or round house (see Figure 39). Early in 1991 Hill left Neshuro, though he occasionally returns to see how the work is progressing, and moved to St Joseph's. This is a community-based and largely community-funded training centre a long way from the tarmac road. It is administered by the local Catholic Church. Here, working alongside carpentry instructor, Steve Morris, he teaches stabilized earth block manufacturing, bricklaying and masonry skills.

## LOW-INCOME BUILDING IN THE CARIBBEAN AND BELIZE

### St Vincent

For two and a half years, from April 1987 until November 1989, development worker Martyn Bennett worked at the Glebe Skills Training Centre at Barrouallie, St Vincent as a skills training instructor. He was responsible for seeing the construction of the training centre through to completion, as well as for his formal training role.

The main training centre buildings were constructed of stabilized earth blocks. David Webb, of the Building Research Establishment (BRE) at Garston, near Watford, Hertfordshire, had been involved in the foundation of the Glebe Skills Training Centre and two BRE Pak block-making presses had been provided as part of the package of assistance for the establishment of the training centre. Martyn Bennett also received some training at BRE in England prior to his departure to St Vincent in 1987. Once the STC buildings were complete, the idea was to use one or both of the BRE Pak block-presses to enable a number of ex-trainees to set up a small block-making business on a site near the STC.

Bennett left St Vincent in May 1989 and, in early 1990, he was replaced by Donncha O'Fionnalaigh who had previously worked as an introductory technology teacher in Nigeria.

O'Fionnalaigh was asked to provide an update on the situation at Barrouallie and find out if anything had become of the idea for a separate block-making business. He reported that the soil-block production unit had not got off the ground. The blocks were used to build the training centre, but the subsequent problems encountered were:

○ Transporting sand from the beach and soil from a different area
○ No site identified to build the workshop on
○ Lack of orders for blocks (some had been expected from the Ministry of Community Development, for example, but these had never materialized) and
○ A pressure gauge on the block press failed and no replacement was available.

He added a number of interesting comments.

It would seem from talking to those who worked on making the blocks that they know the blocks cost less to produce and are stronger than

108

ordinary cavity blocks. And almost everyone admits that they look nicer and therefore don't need to be rendered. The problems with getting the soil block accepted appear to stem from getting people to accept something other than the norm (the cavity block) and trusting the new product when those who are making them don't seem to be fully sure themselves of the correct mixes and thus end up making an inferior product.

O'Fionnalaigh also explained that

although the centre is relatively large, the soil blocks only comprise filling-in between the main timber structure. In other words, the main structure is timber, and I think word got round that the soil blocks were weak as a result. No one told them here that on smaller structures the timber frame was not necessary.

VSO technical postings officer, Keith Budden, who visited Barrouallie in October 1990, added another point. He felt that security of land tenure was a vitally important factor in people's selection of building materials on St Vincent. Sometimes, with a struggle, people who could afford secure land tenure could also afford to build in concrete blocks. On the other hand, if land tenure is not secure and you live in constant fear of eviction at short notice, you will build your house from clapboard, timber and corrugated sheet so that it can be dismantled and re-erected speedily (or even lifted to a new site by hired crane).

## Belize

In 1990, Ian Munt began working on urban planning in Belize City, first with the Belize City Urban Development Corporation (UDC) and then, after the UDCs closure, with the Department of Housing and Planning. The main objective of the UDC was to produce a comprehensive development plan to guide the growth of Belize City, which in 1991 had a rapidly growing population of nearly 60 000, and show how existing problems, such as housing provision, traffic circulation and the environment could be solved.

Munt played a major part in the preparation of a summary of the development plan's aims, for public discussion in Belize. As Belize City was already quite close to the surrounding settlements of Ladyville, Burrell Boom and Hattieville (originally an emergency resettlement camp set up after Hurricane Hattie in 1961), the plan aimed to avoid uncontrolled development on the periphery of Belize City.

The summary puts the case this way:

Areas of land on the edge of the city which are suitable for development must be carefully selected. These areas will be divided into 'phased development units'. For each of these 'phased units', drainage and landfill design schemes and a plan showing how the proposed development will be set out must be drawn up before the development is allowed to go ahead.

Is this rather inflexible, or a top-down approach? The UDC clearly didn't think so. It said: 'This is a highly flexible approach to planning, and it will allow us to respond to changed circumstances. More importantly, new development can be designed and managed by the residents of new neighbourhoods, putting them firmly in control of their future.'

It should be pointed out that the need for organized, infrastructural support and preparation for the establishment of so-called new neighbourhoods was especially high in Belize City because the city is very low-lying and rests, to all intents and purposes, on mangrove swamp. Hence the need for the extensive drainage and landfill referred to in the plan as a precondition for the establishment of healthy living conditions. The UDC recognized that 'it would be cheaper to develop land that did not require landfill and drainage canals, but residents in these areas would face higher transport costs on their journeys into the city'.

Clearly the need to be near to work was a key factor and one which had to be borne in mind if the planners were to have any hope of controlling real development and new building.

On the basis of projected population estimates, it was calculated that about 650 new houses would be needed each year from 1985 to 2010 in the Belize City area with a total land requirement of anything between 556 and 1659 acres, depending on the average plot size which resulted. Special reference was made in the UDCs consultation documents to the need for land to be reserved for housing poorer people. The plan envisaged a combination of credit unions, public and private financing of new housing. The plan also reflected concern for conservation of the environment (protection of marine and mangrove habitats) and of Belize's historic quarters. Munt added that he had no specific involvement with low-cost or self-build housing as such, even though he would have been very interested to work in those fields.

In 1991 there were contradictory signs about which way the Belizean authorities would move on self-build. Some Belizean politicians — like their counterparts the world over — would be reluctant to lose control over the central, municipal allocation of housing, but there were also a number of signs of interest in various low-cost and self-help approaches. Munt continued:

The Housing Section recently returned from Cuba where it was considering the adopting of a self-build, low-cost prefab approach used by the state construction company, UNECA (which also has a lot of activity in Nicaragua). As far as I know, it's still considering either the purchase of the materials or of a plant that makes the prefab sections. Only a mason is required on site in a supervisory capacity. I'm told it's hurricane-proof,

110

looks good when it's finished and only costs approximately half what the state-built homes in Belize currently cost — but, of course, the price will rise due to importation. A recent small scheme in the north of the country used the eventual owners' manual labour as a cost-cutting measure. In addition, of course, many Belizeans lease land (sub-divided) from the government and build when finance is available. It's cheap to lease land — only about $15 Belizean a year in Belize City — and you can purchase land on the completion of a house or dwelling.

## LOW-INCOME BUILDING IN THE PACIFIC

### Fiji

Dave Allen worked as a scheme planner for the Fijian Housing Authority in Suva, Fiji's capital city, from 1989 to 1990. He arrived in July 1989 to work on low-cost housing projects, liaising closely with senior officers in the Housing Authority, the Public Works Department and with officials of the World Bank, who determined the main cost parameters for the whole project, which was dependent on World Bank loans. Significantly, he was not given access to the future users of the low-cost housing.

The specific objectives of his posting were twofold: first to complete planning and design for eight initial sites to be financed under the World Bank Loan scheme; and second, to prepare new concepts of housing layouts which could improve the visual and social aspects of large areas of housing.

Allen commented:

> Possibilities of providing good, low-cost sites for low- or middle-income groups are limited due to land availability and lack of housing subsidy. The Housing Authority being a self-financing organization and the World Bank loan requiring a 15 per cent profit margin is not conducive to providing real quality housing. However, within this framework there are advances to be made in the peri-urban areas for decent settlement and land availability for squatters and 'new families'.

The projects which Allen was working on were so-called site and services projects, that is land was designated for housing development and divided up into individual building plots, with the lines of service roads and walkways marked out. Basic services, such as power, water, drainage and sewerage, were then connected to each lot (or at least to groups of lots, ready for connection to individual lots as construction of actual housing units proceeded).

Allen's assessment continued:

> The sites I have designed this year will, in theory, give rise to over 2000 new plots for house-building over the next four years. Specific design problems are caused by unsuitable, very steep land. The Housing

111

Authority has constantly struggled to make sites on this land viable — the real answer, though, would be acquiring better land, but this is a political issue.

The World Bank required each site to provide serviced plots which would correlate with the percentage distribution of different levels of income-earners within the target groups. To try to work with these restraints and still overcome the problems of topography, Allen submitted a proposal which recommended that two of the sites for development in Suva should be considered as one unit. This would allow greater flexibility in scheme layout in that more of the low-income plots could then be located in areas with easier topography, thus reducing eventual building costs for the householders who could least afford to pay a lot.

Allen made some interesting comments about requirements which he faced to 'relax standards' on these sites:

In many instances, regulations adopted from the UK and New Zealand are inappropriate for low-cost housing in Fiji and deserve to be dropped. However, I am not in favour of enshrining these 'relaxed standards' in more formal regulations. This inevitably leads to a confusion within approval bodies, a retrograde step in national quality and loopholes for abuse by unscrupulous private-sector developers.

At his end of service, in July 1990, Allen produced a 'seven-point plan for reduction in shelter costs'. This is well worth summarizing here. Allen set out his seven points as follows:

○ *Planning* — plan an efficient layout which maximizes the number of units which share services and utilities (road, drainage, toilets, kitchens, and so on)
○ *Materials* — rely on locally-produced materials, assuming that local building material manufacturers will produce materials at lower cost than imports. Thirty per cent savings can be made, and there are other beneficial effects from the use of traditional building materials
○ *Subsystem mix* — omit portions of the shelter that are superfluous or can be upgraded later — this can also mean adaptability of layout for changing family requirements
○ *Infrastructure* — this must be adaptable and upgradable. By spreading cost in this way, immediate on-site costs per unit can be reduced by up to 50 per cent, thereby releasing funds for the preparation of more serviced units
○ *Self-help* — this is to be encouraged. If small, core houses are provided, long-term lease-holders should improve their own dwellings, also providing opportunities for self-expression
○ *Technology* — beware of sophisticated building systems (imported technology, materials and management) as opposed to maximizing the use of a low-tech self-help approach, and

112

○ *House type* — major social and cultural isues are involved here. Be sure to take account of varying family size and make careful assessments of locally-specific, accepted standards of overcrowding and affordability. Provide a range of densities across sites.

**Vanuatu**

We report here on some aspects of the work done by two volunteers who have worked in Vanuatu in recent years — Peter Harris (architect, attached to the Public Works Department, Santo) from 1986 until June 1990 and Tim Etheridge, who has worked for the Ministry of Health, building and refurbishing clinics on small, remote islands, since September 1990.

*Peter Harris, PWD architect, Santo*
Peter Harris arrived in Vanuatu in September 1986. For his first three months there, he stood in for the Public Works Department's principal architect and was based at the PWDs headquarters in Santo, Vanuatu's capital. During that time, he was responsible for all government building projects and gained a good overview of PWDs role.

He then spent 18 months on cyclone construction work, after Cyclone Uma in 1986. He was based on Tanna.

For his final 18 months in the Pacific, he was designated as the regional architect for Vanuatu's northern region. Just before he finished, Ian Patterson, a civil engineer, joined the PWD staff, maintaining VSOs link with the department.

Peter Harris undertook a wide variety of design work during this period of more than three years and worked on designs for the upgrading of nine schools (in Ambae, Maowa, Pentecost and Santo); a fisheries training centre; upgrading of the Santo Air Terminal; a cyclone-relief centre; accommodation blocks for the Departments of Agriculture and Civil Aviation; a number of rain-water catchment structures on Tanna; an Inter-District Games Stadium; and the Operation Centre at Torres. (The latter was a multi-use building which could function as a meeting-house, area council office, rest-house and workshop.)

Sue Wardell, the field director in the Pacific for most of this period, commented:

> Pete clearly demonstrated an appreciation of the necessity to adapt Western design concepts to what is appropriate in the local context. In particular, he actively promoted the use of local materials and components whenever feasible, for example, using round poles, thatch, copra and raffia room-dividing screens on occasion, thereby making his buildings more cost-effective and usually more appropriate in terms of the users.

*Tim Etheridge, building supervisor, Ministry of Health*
Etheridge, who had previously worked as a carpentry instructor at Mazeras Youth Polytechnic, near Mombasa, in Kenya from 1984 to 1986, was posted

to Vanuatu in August 1990. In mid-1989 a thorough survey had been carried out on the state of repair of the structures of health centres and clinics throughout Vanuatu (in the course of which Peter Harris was one of the many people consulted).

Arising from this, VSO was requested by the Minstry of Health to recruit a builder who would be prepared to travel from job to job, often living in fairly basic conditions in remote locations, organizing local workers — some paid, some voluntary — to rehabilitate or rebuild health centres which were in need of major repair and also, where necessary, to carry out improvements to the living quarters allocated for nurses on the various islands, as this would be a major factor in attracting and retaining qualified staff at the various locations. Originally to be based on Tanna, Etheridge's first list of duties included the following jobs:

○ Dillons Bay — extend the existing structure of the health centre to allow for in-patient accommodation and for nurses' accommodation, along with sanitary facilities
○ Futuna — convert and upgrade the existing dispensary into nurses' quarters, construct a new dispensary (described as Type B) and construct toilets
○ Aniwa — as for Futuna, and
○ Imaki — convert/upgrade the existing three-roomed building to nurses' quarters and demolish the decayed and unsafe existing Type A dispensary and construct a new Type B one.

How had things developed a year later? Etheridge said that the work had proceeded according to schedule. He had already built dispensaries on Tanna, Futuna and Aniwa and the first stage of the project was complete. The dispensaries were made from prefabricated sections with structural timber supplied by a Ni-Vanuatu firm, but including imported timber (from Fiji) and roofing sheets (from Australia).

His project was therefore very much along the lines of 'get the job done', focusing on the upgrading of clinics and nurses' accommodation so that medical provision could be improved, rather than aiming specifically to affect local building practices in any way. Etheridge recruited a team of local labourers on each site and then supervised the construction work. He felt that it was frankly not feasible for most aspects of the construction of the buildings he was erecting to be adopted by local people. 'They're out of local people's price range altogether,' said Etheridge. Dwellings in Vanuatu, outside the few towns, were mainly self-built using freely-available local materials such as palm trunks, palm and grass thatch, and copra matting screens.

Etheridge felt that his previous experience as a carpenter in Kenya may not have been all that relevant technically, but he said it was invaluable in helping him to work with local communities and community leaders. Etheridge put it this way: 'Ninety per cent of this job is reaching firm understandings with people and avoiding land disputes.' He felt that he would not have been very well equipped to meet that kind of challenge if it had not been for the time he had spent in Kenya.

CHAPTER FIVE

# *Checklist For Community-Based Builders*

What conclusions can be drawn from the preceding case-studies? Fieldworkers posted to community building projects need to make large professional and personal adaptations. They will be asked to contribute towards the solution of unfamiliar problems using the materials, skills and production processes found locally. Above all they will need to make themselves aware of the social and cultural implications of their work and allow these to guide them at every stage.

Points 1 to 6 below are intended as a checklist for the community builder; they offer guidance, in the context set out in this book, on some of the considerations necessary for a successful community-based building project. Points 7 to 9 suggest a list of techniques or methods for the collection and management of the information required to form hypotheses and develop designs. A successful project will be both a process involving the community in its evolution and a product which is used as the community intends and which will function both technically and socio-culturally in accordance with their requirements.

## 1. First identify the user group

In most groups in which a development worker is involved, the paying client is usually quite different to the user and the requirements of each can also be quite different. The communication between the development worker and the paying client is, certainly at the start of a project, much clearer than that with the user. In order to gain some measure of control over events related to the project, the user group should formulate itself into a committee. The committee should then be able to have regular open meetings to discuss the project, and can communicate with the paying client formally to effect changes which it thinks appropriate. This committee should be involved as far as possible from the inception of the scheme to its completion, and beyond to the running and regular maintenance of the building.

It is to this committee that the development worker can refer to check out ideas and to generate new ones. The user committee can also give accreditation to the development worker, making it easier to gain access to the wider community.

## 2. Study local society and its culture

What sort of society is it? What are its basic needs and how do people go about fulfilling them in work and play? What is the family make-up and how does this affect house form? What is the position of women? What are attitudes to privacy? How and where do people meet, both as individuals and in small or large groups?

What changes are occurring in local society, and what changes do people aspire to for the future? Social and cultural values and aspirations are the most difficult to measure and understand, but have the most profound influence on built form.

### 3. Study local building traditions

Try to find the best examples of local building traditions. Identify the skills and materials that were employed and see if these still exist to the same level. Then look at the range of different types of building and try to categorize them according to materials and techniques and their availability now.

What is the local climate, and how does the local tradition respond to this climate to achieve thermal comfort internally? What building forms seem most appropriate to achieve thermal comfort?

How have people used buildings in the past? How are houses occupied now? What changes are occurring? What can be learnt from these changes?

### 4. Economy

What part does cash play in the economy and how are things bought and sold or exchanged? Is there a tradition of local money-lending? Is it the family who must carry the responsibility for their members in times of trouble, or are there more wide-ranging community institutions who share burdens? Are there more modern economic institutions such as banks or credit unions? How are building workers paid, in cash or in kind, and how does this payment compare with other workers? What proportion of their income does a family normally spend on their home? What might the community user-group reasonably be asked to contribute towards the building-project in cash or labour?

### 5. Use prototypes

The solution of new and unfamiliar problems will often require thinking through from first principles, and then designing, building and testing prototypes. It should not be assumed that architectural drawings are readily understood. Often models will be a more effective communication tool and serve as a focus for group discussion.

New building types such as permanent schools or new building materials such as bricks or blocks should not be introduced into a new context without considerable trepidation as to their likely fit. A great deal of preliminary feasibility assessment of such proposals, followed by the evaluation of new buildings in use should precede any large-scale introduction. Future buildings should be adapted as a result of this evaluation.

117

An analogy for building design might be that of a spiral around a cylindrical core of responses acceptable to the community. Each turn of the spiral represents a conceptual shift. At first, conceptual shifts are made with the help of group discussion of ideas which are presented by the development worker or members of the community. Later, conceptual shifts are made in model, drawing or prototype form as the solution comes within the acceptable range and the building process starts. The views of the users can still effect changes and additions during the process of building and continue after its completion. Figure 40 is a diagram of this process.

Any new technology proposed for inclusion within the building should also be tested as a prototype and improved and adapted as necessary to suit the needs of the user and the demands of the market. This includes technologies such as soil-cement block presses. They may have been used successfully elsewhere but may not suit the context of the particular project. The aim should be for problems to be identified by the user group, and potential solutions to these problems to be tested in context and evaluated by the potential users. The Appendix (see p. 121) provides a checklist and diagram for the designing, building and testing of prototypes in context.

### 6. Use training courses

If a community's participation in the building process is to lead to sustained development, then its lessons need to be disseminated within the wider community. Training not only encourages self-help, but also provides a useful on-going role for government in the cost-effective encouragement of improved building skills and standards. One of the reasons for the preference for traditional and improved traditional technologies by many fieldworkers is this: because of the community's familiarity with such technologies, communication with the development worker and the incorporation of new improved building skills within training programmes is easier.

## NOTES ON METHODS USED FOR THE COLLECTION OF INFORMATION AND THE ACQUISITION OF KNOWLEDGE IN THE FIELD

There is a wide range of literature on the subject of research methodology (Rose 1982 and Leedy 1985), and some on the relationship between design and research (Zeizel 1984). In many ways, design and research are similar, but they are not the same. The results of research are conclusions and recommendations, whereas the results of design are a process or a product. Achievement of knowledge through research is by the formulation and testing of hypotheses. Design knowledge is gained by either the testing of models (either theoretical or actual) or by the construction and testing of prototypes.

Gathering information, whether for research or design, before building work starts, requires similar methods. These are literature research, observation, interview and questionnaire.

## 7. Literature research

Development workers should involve themselves in an extensive literature search both before and after posting. This involves collecting and analyzing information from all available sources in order to gain an insight into the context of the project. The information should cover all the areas mentioned in this book, both technological, economic and socio-cultural. When reading this material care should be taken to examine the historical setting in which an item was written and any perceived bias in the writer.

## 8. Observation and participation

Patient observation of an unfamiliar situation is often a rewarding and enlightening experience. Observation may be a formalized process in which, say, a particular building practice is watched every day for a week. It might be an informal arrangement to live with a family for six months during which careful diary notes are taken, or more likely observation will just be the accumulated experience of the posting.

Perhaps more understanding can be gained, when the time is available, if the observer is also a participant in the practice which is being observed. This is particularly useful where qualitative understanding is being sought rather than just the measurement of quantities. The values that people have, their attitudes and behaviour, are best understood by the participant observer who has the time and inclination to get involved. On the other hand, quantitative information, such as that on prices, strength of materials, or temperature data, can be gathered by more objective and detached methods. Account should be taken by participatory observers of the fact that their involvement will affect the activity, and that in so doing its nature will change to a greater or lesser extent.

## 9. Interviews and questionnaires

Once it is clearer to the development worker and the user committee what the problem is that they are intending to solve, then hypotheses can be developed regarding its solution. Such an hypotheses might be 'we need a house with a thatched roof' or 'all walls should be built of brick'.

These can then be tested using interviews and questionnaires. Clearly, there are some aspects which can be examined using simple questions such as 'what is the price of a brick?' or 'are there suitable grasses or reeds for thatching?'. However, socio-cultural aspects, which are often more important, are usually more difficult to question. Then a set of staged questions might be considered.

The first set of interviews would, most usefully, consist of open questions where the respondent is asked to talk freely about a given subject. 'What do you think is the most suitable type of house for this village?' is a question which might uncover a wide variety of concerns, only some of which would be of relevance to the proposal to build brick walls with thatched roofs.

Once the general opinions of the users on house types have been expressed through such open questions, then more focused interviews based on closed questions such as 'Do you prefer brick or block walls?' or 'If the fibre-cement tiles are coloured red, would you prefer them to thatch?' can be carried out.

All the above techniques of research have limited applicability. A researcher must always be clear as to the scope and scale of the sample. If the questions are too wide and general, then the applicability of the results in a particular place will be in doubt. If they are too specific and narrow in their vision, then they will not be generally relevant.

The possession of good communication skills by the development worker is essential to the task of community building in relation to research techniques, encouraging user-participation in design, liaison with the user committee and training programmes. Once there is a firm proposal, this must be presented and understood by the user committee in the form of drawings and models so that final changes can be made before starting on site. Once work does start on site, the hypotheses which have been tested in theory in interviews and within the user committee are replaced by the prototype building which is to be tested in use.

# Designing, Building and Testing Prototypes

## THE PROBLEM-SOLVING PROCESS

1.00 **Identify problem:**

1.01 as seen by local people;
1.02 as seen by local government;
1.03 as seen by aid agency.

2.00 **Establish boundaries:**

2.01 local social and economic conditions;
2.02 own time and ability;
2.03 project resources;
2.04 what other resources could be acquired.

3.00 **List range of possible solutions** in theory and identify their constraints, including socio-economic, and organizational constraints. It should be noted that a prototype solution may not be exclusively technical but can also be organizational or financial. For each technical solution proposed:

3.01 do you understand the scientific principles involved?
3.02 what local or imported materials are available and at what price?
3.03 identify properties of materials available by test, from literature, and by observing local use;
3.04 what skills are available locally?
3.05 what skills will be new and can they be easily acquired?
3.06 what side-effects will your solutions have?

4.00 **Design, build, test and assess prototypes**

4.01 discuss, demonstrate, and involve local users;
4.02 does it work?

*If yes:*

4.03 does it solve the problem?
4.04 is it the simplest solution?
4.05 is it safe and reliable?
4.06 will it last long enough?
4.07 can this first design be improved?

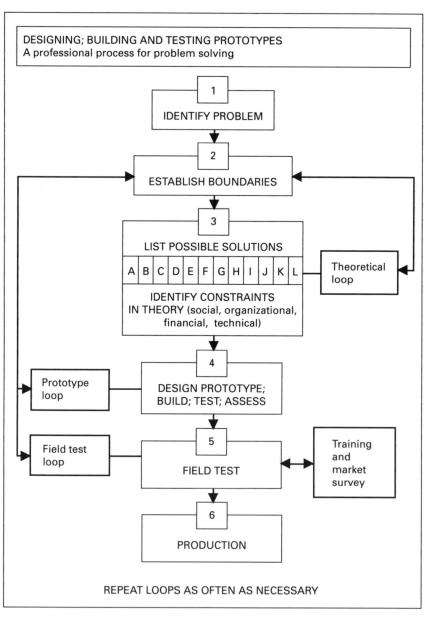

Figure 40. *Diagram of prototype development used for VSO training courses (after Garman and Mitchell, 1987).*

*If no:*

4.08    does the problem still appear solvable at this technical level or must you start again from 2.00 or 3.00 above?

5.00    **Field-test successful prototype:**

5.01    construct several units for extended field test;
5.02    is the solution really appropriate for the users?
5.03    does it work under field conditions?
5.04    do you need to modify the product (if yes, return to 4.00 above)?

*Establish training programme:*

5.05    set up training for makers, builders, installers, users.

*Carry out market survey:*

5.06    how widespread is the application for this product?
5.07    what price would people pay for it?
5.08    is it worth setting up production or must you start again at 2.00, 3.00 or 4.00 above?

6.00    **Set up production:**

6.01    can local facilities cope with the demand?
6.02    what additional resources will be required (e.g. training, management, marketing, currency)?
6.03    what will be the effect when you leave?
6.04    what disadvantages will the introduction of the product have and how will you and the local community deal with them?
6.05    what advantages will the introduction of the product have and how will you and the local community deal with them?

# Postscript: Some lessons for us all?

In the introduction to this book, we referred to the opportunities for learning and for gaining new insights into the application of skills which work in a developing country can often provide for an architect or builder who has been trained in the West. By way of some concluding thoughts, we would like to return to that very point. Frankly, we believe that there are many crucial ways in which we could improve the practices of the building community in Britain by learning from aspects of the traditional, community-based self-help building approach used by many peoples in Africa, Asia and the Pacific.

In the process of the Industrial Revolution in the West, the shift to urban life and machine manufacture led to the decline of rural skills such as building in cob, wattle and daub, hurdling, and thatching. At the same time, along with the loss of these traditional, rural building skills, we largely lost the self-build tradition too. It has been replaced by huge advances in our knowledge of materials and structural engineering and by specialization in the building trades and professions, by increasingly complex and demanding regulations, and by a specialist housing market, serviced by an army of estate agents, solicitors and conveyancers. It is a process controlled by experts.

Consequently, even those individual citizens who have the necessary funds to become players in the housing market have very little say in the process of housing themselves — typically, they are disempowered and kept at arms' length from the whole process. As for those who lack the necessary funds, they may well end up homeless or, at best, living in severely inadequate housing.

This contrasts sharply with our (admittedly idealized) picture of the African village where the chief allocates land by right and where a farmer can build his own house, determining its size and, within customary limits, its design, with a little help from neighbours and relatives, without any of the complications and obstacles facing the would-be householder in the West. In this setting, housing is clearly seen as a right and as a fundamentally natural, social activity. Meeting the need for housing then becomes a natural part of the cycle of life.

In the West, on the other hand, there is very little, if any, community choice in the field of housing. People are not, as a rule, involved in the design and building of their own accommodation. As a result, we have seen such blind alleys as the high-rise system-building solutions to urban housing need, which have been adopted in some Third World cities too. In Britain, some of these high-rise blocks are now being dynamited as they have proved to be unsuitable for human accommodation. Along with these high-cost, high-rise solutions has gone the break-up of entire urban communities and the spread of urban vandalism.

The housing unit has become a mere commodity. It is not seen, in any way, as the outcome of human involvement and activity for the occupier at all.

It is true to say that the self-build movement of recent years has begun to emerge from the fringes of alternative society, along with other types of movement stressing consumer choice, and building on older traditions of rural self-help (and the Plotlands movement of the 1920s and 1930s for example), but it is still very much a tiny minority phenomenon.

Maybe there is a fundamental human urge to build, to house oneself, to provide shelter. As we are alienated from that in modern, industrial society, more and more people seem to spend their leisure time on therapeutic DIY, restoration and refurbishment!

So we see a spectrum. Without too much idealization we can describe it thus. At one end, there is rural Africa with its technical options limited by traditionally available materials, skills and customary design but with a complete involvement by each householder in the housing process. At the other end of the spectrum, we have the West, with almost unlimited technical and economic options but the nearly complete exclusion of the householder from the housing process. Is some kind of reciprocal learning process desirable, or even possible, here? We believe the answer must be yes if housing is seen as a fundamentally social process, necessary to people's well-being, rather than just an exercise in the mass-production of yet another commodity.

# Bibliography

Action-Aid Kenya 'Action Pack Block Press', information sheet, Appropriate Technology Unit (undated).

Agarwal, A., *Mud, mud: the potential of earth-based materials for Third World housing*, Earthscan, 1981.

Al-Azzawi, S.H., 'Oriental Houses in Iraq' in Oliver, P., (ed.) *Shelter and Society*, Barrie and Rockliff, 1969.

Alexander, C., *Notes on the Synthesis of Form*, Harvard University Press, 1970.

Barbour, K.M., *The Republic of the Sudan, A Regional Geography*, University of London Press, 1961.

Bilbeisi, Z., 'The effects of Permanent Architecture on the Socio-Cultural Values of Al-Badu (in Jordan)', Ph.D. proposal to Cambridge University, 1990.

Birch, L., *Training Programmes for Low-Cost Housing*, Pergamon Press, 1981.

Bourdier, J.P., 'Houses of Light', in *MIMAR; Architecture in Development*, No. 39, 1991.

Bouverie, J., 'Recycling in Cairo: a tale of rags to riches', in *New Scientist*, No. 1775, 29 June 1991.

Brunskill, R.W., *The Illustrated Handbook of Vernacular Architecture*, Faber and Faber, 1978.

Building Research Establishment, *Building in Hot Climates: A selection of Oversees Building Notes* (contains list of Building Research Centres throughout the world), Dept. of the Environment, 1980.

Building Research Establishment, *The Multibloc BREPAK Block Press*, promotional literature, BRE, Dept. of the Environment, 1982.

Bullard, C. and Tunley, P., *Domes not Doums — a case study: the introduction of earth brick domes and vaults to the Oullam region of Niger*, Development Workshop, 1982.

Burgess, R., 'Petty Commodity Housing or Dweller Control? A Critique of John Turner's Views on Housing Policy', in *World Development*, 1978, pp. 1105–33.

Daldy, A.F., *Temporary Buildings in Northern Nigeria*, Government Printer, Lagos, 1945.

Dawson, J., *Using Technical Skills in Community Development* (ed. Ball, M.), VSO (ECOE programme), 1990.

Denyer, S., *African Traditional Architecture*, Heinemann, 1978.

Development Workshop, *The introduction to Niger of Nubian Domes and Vaults*, 1990.

Drewer, S., 'Institutional Constraints to the Choice of Appropriate Construction Technology', working paper, International Labour Organization, 1982.

Duly, C., *The Houses of Mankind*, Thames and Hudson, 1979.

Duncan, J.S., (ed.), *Housing and Identity*, Holmes and Meier, 1982.

Edwards, M., (ed.), *Arriving Where We Started; 25 years of Voluntary Service Overseas*, VSO and IT Publications, 1983.

Fathy, H., *Architecture for the Poor*, University of Chicago Press, 1973.

Forty, A., 'Problems in the History of a Profession: Architecture in Britain in the Nineteenth and Early Twentieth Centuries', unpublished paper, University College, London (undated).

Francis, A.J., *The Cement Industry 1796–1914: A History*, David & Charles, 1977.

Fry, M. and Drew, J., *Tropical Architecture*, Batsford, 1964.

Garman, P. and Mitchell, M., 'Technical Training for Overseas', VSO, 1987.

Greenstreet, R., 'Investigation and analysis of the structure of the building control process', Ph.D. thesis, Oxford Polytechnic, 1983.

Hammer, D. and Tunley, P., *Iferouane — Habitat en evolution*. Development Workshop, (IUCN/WWF), 1991.

Hardoy, J. and Satterthwaite, D., *Shelter: Need and Response*, Wiley, 1982.

Hardoy, J. and Satterthwaite, D., *Housing and Health. Do Architects and Planners Have a Role?* Reprinted by IIED from *Cities*, Vol. 4, No. 3, 1987.

Hardoy, J. and Satterthwaite, D., *Squatter Citizen*, Earthscan, 1989.

Hardy, D. and Ward, C., *Arcadia for All: The Legacy of a Makeshift Landscape*, Mansell, 1984.

HMG Nepal, *Outline of an Action Plan for the Reconstruction and Rehabilitation of Earthquake Affected Schools*, MHPP-EAARRP, Kathmandu, 1988.

Hockings, J., 'Built Form and Culture: A Theoretical Appraisal Supported by a Case Study of the Dwelling House in the Gilbert Islands, West Pacific Ocean', in *Architecture and Comfort/Architectural Behaviour*, Vol. 3, No. 4, 1987, pp. 281–300.

Huybers, P., *Manual on the Delft Wire Lacing Tool*, Delft University of Technology, 1984.

Huybers, P. and Groot, C.J.W.P., *Survey of Activities in the Field of Building Technology for Developing Countries*, Delft University of Technology, 1983.

Illich, I., (ed.), *Disabling Professions*, Marion Boyars, 1977.

Intermediate Technology Development Group, Kenya *Building Regulations and Bye-Laws*, ITDG Kenya, 1989.

Ive, G., 'A contribution to a review and agenda for research into the production of the built environment in (former British colonial) Africa', paper given at Bartlett International Summer School, 1985.

King, A.D., *The Bungalow*, Routledge Kegan and Paul, 1984.

Koenigsberger, O.H. *et al*, *Manual of Tropical Housing and Building: Part One: Climatic Design*, Longman, 1974.

Leedy, P.D., *Practical Research, Planning and Design*, Macmillan, 1985.

Little, K., *West African Urbanization. A study of Voluntary Associations in Social Change*, Cambridge University Press, 1970.

Litvinoff, M., *Earthscan Action Handbook*, Earthscan, 1990.

Lloyd, M., 'Zoning Regulations, Towards a More Flexible Basis', a discussion document for the Ministry of Municipal and Rural Affairs and the Deputy Ministry of Town Planning, Saudi Arabia, 1986.

Meadows, Randers, Behrens, *Limits to Growth*, Pan, 1972.

Menard, H.W., *Geology Resources and Society: An Introduction to Earth Science*, W.H. Freeman, 1974.

Mitchell, M., 'An attempt at describing the situation of Tinezouline in 1968', unpublished report to the Architectural Association, 1969.

Mitchell, M., 'Shanty Cash', report submitted to Architectural Association for Bristol award, 1975.

Mitchell, M., 'Rehabilitation activities in Thanh Hoa Province following typhoon Irving — Report of Mission to Thanh Hoa', Development Workshop and GRET, unpublished report to United Nations Centre for Human Settlements, 1990.

Moore, A., *How to make twelve woodworking tools*, IT Publications, 1986.

Moore, A., *How to make planes, cramps and vices*, IT Publications, 1987.

Moser, C.O.N. and Peake, L., (eds.) *Women, Human Settlements, and Housing*, Tavistock, 1987.

Moughtin, J.C., 'Settlements and housing in an arid-zone developing country: case study in Hausaland, Northern Nigeria' in Oliver, P., (ed.) *Shelter and Society*, Barrie and Rockliff, 1969.

Moughtin, J.C., *Hausa Architecture*, Ethnographica, London, 1985.

Okie, J.S., *Block Press Handbook*, University of Science and Technology, Kumasi, Ghana, 1971.

Oliver, P., (ed.), *Shelter in Africa*, Barrie and Jenkins, 1971.

Oliver, P., *Dwellings: The House Across the World*, Phaidon, Oxford, 1987.

Ongom, J., 'Changing Social Structure and Built Form in Ghana', M.Sc. report, University College, London, 1990.

Pellow, D., 'What Housing Does: Changes in an Accra Community', in *Architecture and Comfort/Architectural Behaviour*, Vol. 4, No. 3, 1988.

Rapoport, A., *House Form and Culture*, Prentice-Hall, 1969.

Rapoport, A. *The meaning of the built environment: a non-verbal communication approach*, Sage, Beverly Hills, 1982.

Rodwin, L. (ed.), *Shelter, Settlement and Development*, Allen and Unwin, 1987.

Rose, G., *Deciphering Sociological Research*, Macmillan, 1982.

Said, E.W., *Orientalism*, Peregrine Books, 1985.

Salas, J. 'An Analysis of Latin American Auto-Construction: A Plural and Mass Phenomenon', in *Open House International*, Vol. 13, no. 4, 1988.

Schumacher, D., 'Energy for Human Shelter within the Global Shelter: Energy Policy Planning in the Third World', in *Homes Above All*, The Building and Social Housing Foundation, Coalville, Leicestershire, 1987.

Schuman, T., 'The Agony and the Equity: A Critique of Self-Help Housing', in Bratt *et al.* (ed.) *Critical Perpsectives on Housing*, Temple University Press, 1986.

Sigurdson, J., *Small-Scale Cement Plants*, ITDG, 1977.

Spence, R.J.S., (undated) *Making Soil-Cement Blocks*, University of Zambia.

Spence, R.J.S. and Cook, D.J., *Building Materials in Developing Countries*, Wiley, 1983.

Thesiger, T. *The Marsh Arabs*, Penquin 1967.

Turner, J.F.C. and Fitcher, R., (eds) *Freedom to Build*. Macmillan, New York, 1972.

Turner, J.F.C., *Housing By People*, Marion Boyars, 1976.

Turner, J.F.C., 'Why Work with People?' and 'The Challenge of Enablement: Tasks for Architects' in Das, S.K. (ed.) *The Architect as Enabler of User House Planning and Design*, International Union of Architects (UIA), 1984.

UNCHS (Habitat) *Survey of Slum and Squatter Settlements*, UNHCS (Habitat), 1982.

UNEP 'Scientific Assessment of Climate Change', the policymaker's summary of the report of Working Groups I and II to the Intergovernmental Panel on Climate Change, WMO and UNEP, 1990.

Ward, P.M., (ed.), *Self-Help Housing — A Critique*, Mansell, 1982.

Zeizel, J., *Inquiry by Design*, Cambridge University Press, 1984.

# THE ECOE PROGRAMME

(Evaluating and Communicating our Overseas Experience)

## THE NEED

Over the past thirty years, more than 20,000 volunteers have worked abroad with VSO. Currently, there are over 1,200 volunteers working in over 40 developing countries in Africa, Asia, the Pacific and the Caribbean for periods of two years or more. However, we have become increasingly aware that much of this valuable experience has been lost through not being recorded in ways which make it accessible and communicable. The ECOE Programme addresses this problem.

## THE AIM

The aim is to record volunteers' experience in reports, videos, seminars, conferences, books, etc. This body of knowledge supplements and supports the work of individual volunteers. It also provides information which is accessible not only to volunteers but also to their employers overseas and to other agencies for whom the information is relevant. Care is taken to present each area of volunteer experience in the context of current thinking about development so that VSO both contributes to development discussions and learns lessons from them for the continuance of its work.

## ADVISORY PANEL

A panel of opinion leaders in relevant professions and in development thinking advises on the selection and commissioning of ECOE publications.

For further information write to:

The Programme Evaluation Manager
VSO
317 Putney Bridge Road
London SW15 2PN, UK
Tel: 081–780 2266   Fax: 081–780 1326